The Mesa Site:
Paleoindians above the Arctic Circle

Michael Kunz
Michael Bever
Constance Adkins

BLM-Alaska Open File Report 86
April 2003

U. S. Department of the Interior

Mammoth and American Lion: A Late Ice Age Scene from the Brooks Range, Arctic Alaska
(Taken from a painting by George "Rinaldino" Teichmann)

CONTENTS

FIGURES

ACKNOWLEDGMENTS

The Bureau of Land Management, Fairbanks District, Arctic District, and Northern Field Office provided the funding for the field work and analysis associated with the Mesa archaeological project. We thank John Santora, Robert Gal, and Carl Johnson for their support of our efforts during the early years of the project. More recently a special thanks to Dixie Swanson for continuous assistance with personnel matters. We also thank Billy Butts, Dee Ritchie, and Dick Bouts for their efforts on behalf of the project and Susan Will for her unflagging encouragement for the completion of this report. Other entities and personnel were also critical to the successful completion of the project and we recognize them here in no particular order.

The excavation of the Mesa Site required 13 field seasons, which were spread over a period of 22 years. The most necessary element of the work, the excavation crews, were comprised of paid personnel as well as highly experienced volunteers. Over the years these crews accounted for a large number of people. Because of this some individuals deserving of recognition have undoubtedly been overlooked. To those people we express our most sincere apologies and our gratitude.

Crew Members

1978   Michael Kunz, Dale Slaughter, Peter Bowers, Susan Will.
Helicopter pilot — Michael Plantz

1979   Susan Will, Peter Bowers, Tim Smith, Georgeie Reynolds, Michael Kunz.
Helicopter pilot — Rick Griffith

1980   Peter Bowers, Michael Kunz, Richard Reanier.
Helicopter pilot — Bill Murphy

1989   Michael Kunz, Richard Reanier, John Cook.

1991   Valerie Gaston, Charles Adkins, Michael Kunz.
Helicopter pilot — Mike Arleen

1992   Sergei Slobodin, Richard Reanier, Michael Kunz, Susan Reanier, Eric Dillingham, Annalisa McGlinn, Dan Gullickson.
Helicopter pilot — Jim Scroggins

1993   Charles Adkins, Susan Reanier, Sergei Slobodin, Richard Reanier, Daniel Mann, Michael Kunz.
Helicopter pilot — Rick Farish

1994   Susan Reanier, Lara Fedor-Ziady, Kellie Cairns, Michael Bever, Eric Dillingham, Michael Kunz, Richard Reanier, Dennis Stanford, Daniel Mann, Peggy Jodry.
Helicopter pilot — Garland Dobbins

1995   Kellie Cairns, Leslie Cook, Connie Adkins, Sergei Slobodin, Kristen Wenzel, Michael Bever, Michael Kunz.
Helicopter pilot — Don Willey

1996   Michael Bever, Robert Godsoe, Kristen Wenzel, Gordon Karg, Robert Watson Connie Adkins, Michael Kunz, Stephen Durand, Richard Reanier, Daniel Mann, Dorothy Peteet, David Meltzer, Robert Fox, Tom Reanier
Helicopter pilot — Mark Fleming

1997   Connie Adkins, Robert Godsoe, Joshua Reuther, Amber Lincoln, Susan Reanier, Richard Reanier, Kristen Wenzel, Robert Watson, Susan Will, Stephen Durand, Daniel Mann, Dorothy Peteet, Angela Wittenberg, Michael Kunz, Lawrence Plug, Kaarin Tae, Patricia Heiser, Carolyn Parker, Charles Adkins.
Helicopter pilots — Bill Murphy, Ed Bartoli
Helicopter mechanic — Lowell Berentsen

1998   Robert Godsoe, Wynola Possenti, Connie Adkins, Michael Bever, John Dubé, Joshua Reuther, Paul Matheus, Daniel Mann, Michael Kunz, Pamela Groves, Julie Chase.
Helicopter pilot — Bill Murphy
Helicopter mechanic — Glenn Hamilton

1999   Angela Wittenberg, John Dubé, Connie Adkins, Catherina Omtzigt, Paul Matheus, Daniel Mann, Heather McDonald, Michael Kunz, Pamela Groves.
Helicopter pilot — Dave Mason
Helicopter mechanic — Steve Brown

Without the assistance of the Bureau of Land Management's Alaska Fire Service, the Mesa archaeological project could not have been conducted. We especially wish to thank the warehouse personnel who filled our equipment and supply orders and helped in numerous other ways as well. The staff of the Alaska Interagency Coordination Center provided us with excellent logistical support, acquired aircraft for us, and provided flight following, as well as other operational assistance. The Alaska Smokejumpers provided us with field personnel and paracargo support. We thank the Fire Specialists Section for detailing personnel to assist us in the field. The Fuel Specialists established excellent remote aircraft fueling sites for us and the Information Systems and Communications personnel provided us with a reliable communications network. We also wish to thank all of the air and ground crews and office personnel for their efforts in our behalf.

There were several fixed-wing pilots who contributed substantially over the years to our logistical endeavors. We would like to thank Sherpa pilots, Randy Slayton and C. R. Holder; Caravan pilots, Jay Worley, Mick Van Hatten, and Terrell Bailey; Casa Pilots, Kevin and K. T. McBride; and Aero Commander pilots, Doug Montgomery and Fritz R. Hansen. We would also like to extend our profound thanks to our Alaska Fire Service loadmasters, Don Bell and George Rainey.

Additional support and assistance was provided by ARCO Alaska Inc., the University of Alaska Fairbanks, the North Slope Borough, Ilisagvik College and the Polar Ice Coring Office. The authors would especially like to thank Daniel Mann, Paul Matheus, Pamela Groves, Steve Durand, Gill Mull, Bruce Hardy, Robert Watson, Beth Shapiro, and Richard Reanier for their assistance and significant contributions to this report. We also thank George Frison, Vance Haynes, Phil Shelly, Tony Baker, Bruce Bradley, Dennis Stanford, Peggy Jodry, David Meltzer, Jeff Rasic, Robert Ackerman, Ruthann Knudson, Bruce Huckle, Julie Morrow, Peter Bostrom, Alan Cooper, Dale Slaughter, and John Cook for their helpful discussions. Thanks to Lenore Heppler and Stan Bloom for assistance with illustrations. A special thanks goes to Robin Mills, Howard Smith, Angela Wittenberg, Charles Adkins, Pricilla Hammon, Alison Boyce and Tony Baker for reviewing the manuscript and providing numerous helpful suggestions. Finally, given the extended amount of time we spent in the field, we would like to thank all the families of all the crews for their support of our absences and for welcoming us home warmly when we did return.

ABSTRACT

Between 1978 and 1999, excavations in arctic and western Alaska have revealed the presence of Paleoindians during terminal Pleistocene/early Holocene times, ca. 12,000 to 9500 years BP (Before Present). The Type Site for this cultural manifestation, the Mesa Site, is located on the northern flank of the central Brooks Range at N68° 24.72 W155° 48.02, amid rolling foothills that extend northward 40 miles to the Colville River. The site lies atop a mesa-like ridge that rises 180 feet above the floor of the Iteriak Creek valley, offering an unobstructed 360° view of the surrounding treeless countryside. Excavation at the site has produced the remains of more than 450 formal flaked stone tools and over 120,000 pieces of lithic debitage, which comprise an assemblage typical of the "classic" Paleoindian cultures of the North American High Plains. More than 150 of the artifacts are the complete or fragmentary remains of lanceolate projectile points, many of which have been recovered from within the charcoal/soil matrix of discrete hearths which are the central features of numerous activity areas. The age of the occupation is constrained by 44 uncalibrated AMS radiocarbon dates covering the interval 11,700 to 9700 years BP. The site lacks evidence of any widespread postdepositional disturbance and, except for a small, discrete manifestation in Locality A, contains no remains of more recent cultures. The composition of the Mesa artifact assemblage and its obvious technological relationship with the Paleoindian cultures of mid-continent North America mark it as distinctly different from other ancient arctic cultures. The presence of the Mesa Complex demonstrates a previously undocumented cultural diversity in Eastern Beringia at the Pleistocene/ Holocene boundary.

Vulpes vulpes (fox) watches John Dubé and Angela Wittenberg excavating at the Mesa.
(Photo: M. Kunz)

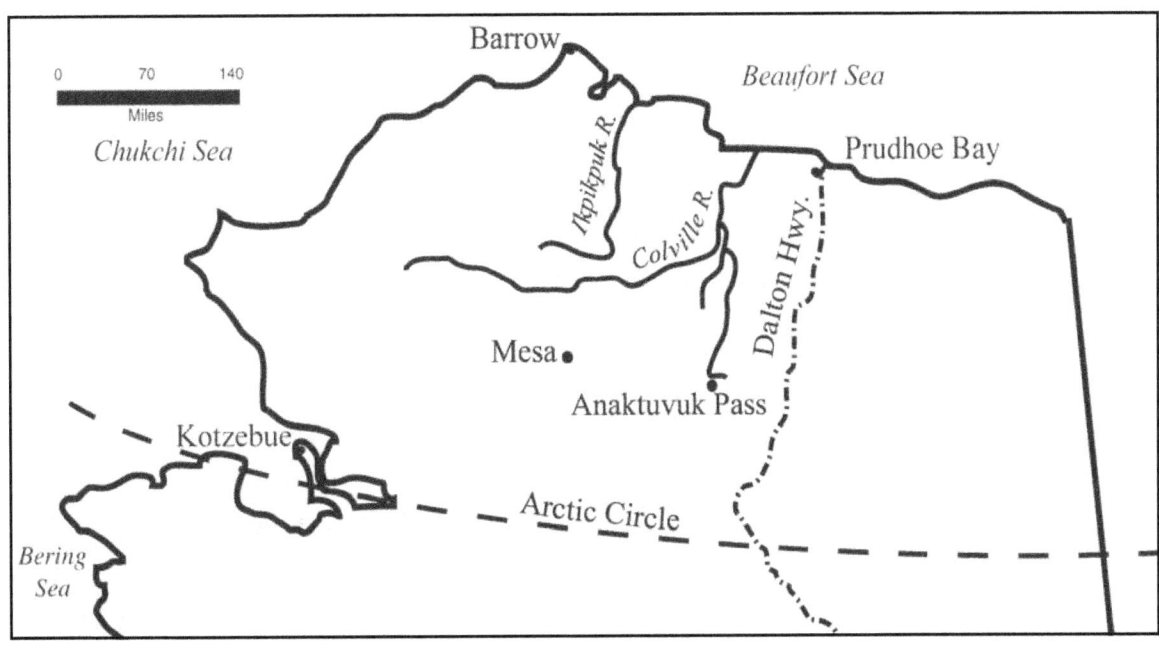

Figure 1. Mesa located in arctic Alaska.

FORWARD

The Mesa archaeological site lies nearly 150 miles above the Arctic Circle in arctic Alaska. The closest village, Anaktuvuk Pass, is more than 100[1] miles to the east-southeast. The nearest road, the Dalton Highway, is 160 miles to the east, and the closest town, Barrow, lies 200 miles to the north on the shore of the Arctic Ocean (Figure 1). The sign at the Ivotuk airstrip, six miles north of the Mesa states, "When You Are Here, You're Still Nowhere." Even in a land where just about anywhere is only reachable by air or water transportation, to say that the Mesa is isolated and remote is an understatement.

All primary logistical operations required fixed-wing aircraft, and the 5000-foot long

---

[1] The English measurement system was used to set up the original site grid and is used throughout this report. Artifact dimensions are the exception using the metric system.

Figure 2. Helicopter slinging equipment to Mesa campsite. (Photo: M. Kunz)

Figure 3 & 3a. Parachuting fuel, three 55-gallon drums to a pallet, to a remote fuel site. (Photos: C. M. Adkins)

gravel airstrip at Ivotuk. Built for oil and gas exploration activities in the late 1970s, the proximity of this airstrip made it possible for us to fly all our personnel, equipment, gear, and supplies to within six miles of the site, and then use a helicopter for transport to the Mesa (Figure 2). To establish helicopter fueling sites remote from Ivotuk we had to parachute 55-gallon drums, usually three to a pallet (Figure 3) from aircraft. Occasionally, when our helicopter was not available, we received supplies by low-level free-fall air drop. In terms of any type of communication other than satellite, the Mesa is in a black hole. Prior to the 1990s, communication with the outside world was tenuous at best. To be able to maintain continuous communication with

Figure 4. Looking north at Mesa Camp and the Mesa. (Photo: M. Kunz)

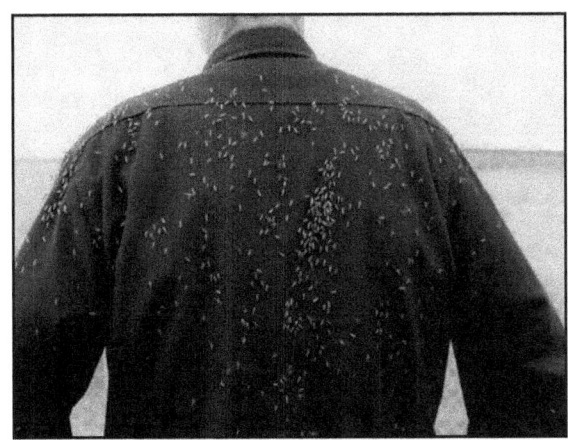

Figure 5. Mosquitoes clustering on the downwind side of an excavator's shirt on a warm day at the Mesa. (Photo: C.M. Adkins)

aircraft within our area of operations (a 200 mile radius of the Mesa), we had to set up a radio repeater system. In emergency situations, response time for any remedial action beyond our own capabilities was a minimum of six hours, if the weather was good. If the weather was bad, it could be days.

Mesa Camp was a tent camp in the strictest sense of the word (Figure 4). Each crew member had a small dome tent for sleeping and personal privacy, while wall tents and other canvas structures provided storage, kitchen/dining, and laboratory space. Sanitation was provided by pit and propane-fired incinerator toilets. Snow excavated from the remnants of large winter drifts provided our refrigeration, and water came from a nearby creek. Bathing was achieved by filling a portable shower unit with water heated on the stove. All in all, it was fairly comfortable. Most of our discomforts resulted from the hordes of mosquitos (Figure 5), occasional snow storms and other adverse weather. Our major safety concern was keeping an eye open for the local grizzly bears so as to avoid confrontations and to keep them out of camp. The grizzlies that were determined to enter camp we were able to chase off with our helicopter, and as a result never had to shoot one.

Wildlife abounds in the area. Foxes regularly raised families in dens excavated into the Mesa's talus slopes, and the sheer rock faces of the Mesa provided nesting habitat for gyrfalcons and rough-legged hawks. Wolves occasionally passed through camp, and often we were surrounded by hundreds or thousands of caribou. (Figure 6) All this, accompanied by 24-hour daylight, made the Mesa project much more than just another archaeological excavation. All of the crew members and visitors to the site enjoyed these unique wilderness circumstances and experiences.

Figure 6. Caribou near Iteriak Creek adjacent to the Mesa. (Photo: P.M. Bowers)

INTRODUCTION
Purpose of the Report

This is an interim report. The amount of data generated by the Mesa project is immense. Although we engaged in some analysis and compilation of data as we progressed through the field work, we are not in a position to present this information in its totality. Therefore, limits have necessarily been placed upon the scope of this report so that it can be completed in a reasonable amount of time. While some primary analysis has not been completed, we have enough information to present a report that is more descriptive and introspective than a raw data monograph. In this report, we will address the scope of research, order and describe the data analyzed so far, and interpret and summarize the findings to date. This will be accomplished by discussing the following subjects: the culture history of the region and the place of the Mesa Complex within that culture history framework; the natural setting of the site region; the excavation and data collection methods; the description of the site including the natural and cultural stratigraphy, cultural features, localities and activity areas; the flaked stone industry including artifact typology, tool-stone variety, and tool use; the regional Pleistocene faunal assemblage; the regional Pleistocene climate and ecology; and site use.

The Culture History of Arctic Alaska

For the purposes of this report, arctic Alaska is defined as that portion of Alaska north of the Continental Divide, or that area north of the 68th degree of latitude (Figure 7). The culture history of arctic Alaska differs significantly from the culture history of other regions of North America in that its earliest human residents appear to be the first people to have set foot in the Western Hemisphere. The physical remains of at least 12,000 years of human occupation appear to be present within arctic Alaska, and it is the only place where the prehistoric culture history of the New World can be traced from its beginning to the present

Figure 7. Location of Mesa in the regional landscape in arctic Alaska. (After Mann et al. 2002)

day. Given that much of the ancient subcontinent of Beringia[2] now comprises the floor of the Beaufort, Chukchi, and Bering Seas, the initial chapter of the culture history of the region is somewhat speculative (Figure 8).

Most archaeologists would probably agree that the region was initially occupied by immigrants from Asia who crossed the land bridge from Siberia to Alaska ca. 15,000 years BP (Radiocarbon Years Before Present), and that some time before 11,500 years BP their descendants moved south and populated the rest of the Western Hemisphere.

The archaeological record indicates that the lithic industry of the Asian immigrants was based on core and blade technology typified by the production of unifacial tools such as burins and worked blades, although some bifacial tools were also produced (Dikov 1977, 1979, 1996, 1997).

There is little doubt that the various cultural groups involved in the earliest migrations into the North American Arctic were deterred from moving south by any route because of the mass of glacial ice that isolated Eastern Beringia (Alaska) from the

---

[2] Beringia existed during the glacial episodes of the Pleistocene when world-wide sea level was as much as 300 feet lower than today. Beringia included most of northeastern Siberia, Alaska as far south as the Alaska Peninsula, and the land bridge that connected them. This was a vast, mostly unglaciated land mass of nearly two million square miles with an extreme continental climate (see Hopkins 1982).

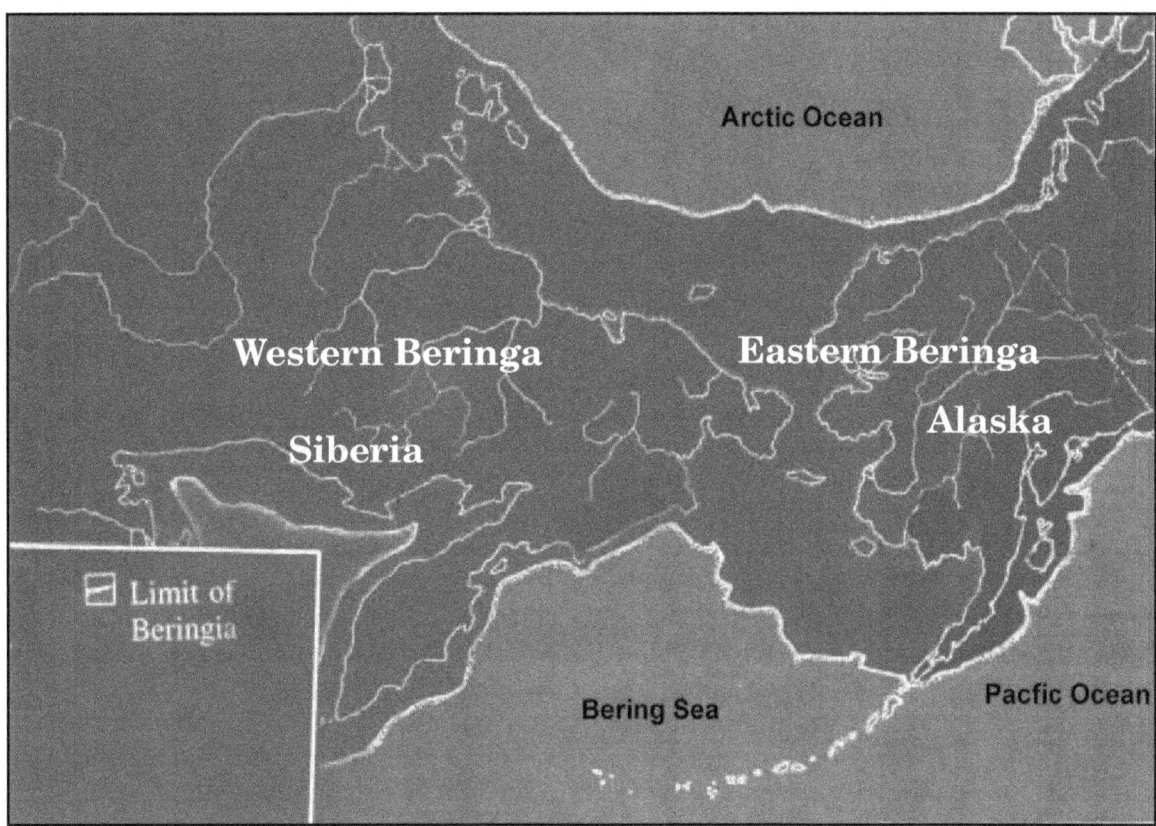

Figure 8. Map of Beringia. (Map: M. King)

rest of the North American continent (Mann and Hamilton 1995; Kunz 1996; Mandryk, et al, 1998, 2001). While contained in unglaciated but ice-bound Eastern Beringia, we believe that some of these people developed a lithic technology specific to the procurement of large mammals, most probably bison and caribou. These tools included large, bifacial, lanceolate projectile points, bifacial knives, and distinctive unifacial tools such as scrapers and gravers. If so, as defined by technology and culture, these people would have been the first Paleoindians. At the same time other immigrant groups retained core and blade technology, but they appear to have occupied the region south of the Continental Divide.

Until recently Paleoindians were not recognized in arctic Alaska. They were originally noted in 1926 more than 3000 miles to the south at Folsom, New Mexico. Since the middle of the last century, Paleoindians have been considered by most scholars to represent the first indigenous, geographically widespread, North American cultural

tradition (Kunz and Reanier 1995).

As the climate and vegetational regime began to change at the end of the Pleistocene, and the large Ice Age mammals such as bison disappeared, the Paleoindians vanished from arctic Alaska's archaeological record. In fact, from roughly 9700 until 7500 years BP there is no solid evidence for human occupation in arctic Alaska (Kunz et al. 2000.) So ends the first chapter of arctic Alaska's culture history.

The loosely defined, technologically Western Beringian affiliated, Paleo-Arctic tradition, which must be as ancient as the Paleoindian tradition, is found nearby on the south side of the Continental Divide (Anderson 1970). Although some researchers (Anderson 1970; Bowers 1982; Gal 1982) have suggested that a few sites derived from the Paleo-Arctic tradition are present north of the Brooks Range, the tradition's lack of diagnostic artifacts and the absence of radiocarbon dates render the reality uncertain at best. However, given that the boundary that separates arctic Alaska from the area to the south is little more than a line we've drawn on a map for our convenience, the Paleo-Arctic tradition may well be part of arctic Alaska's culture history. Because of its ephemeral nature (it is defined and described differently by various researchers) it is difficult to determine an end date for this cultural tradition (Anderson 1970; Dumond, 1987; Goebel et al. 1991). However the general consensus is that the end came around 8000 years BP.

The Paleoindian and Paleo-Arctic cultures were followed by the people of the Northern Archaic tradition (Anderson 1968). This archaeological grouping is present in arctic Alaska from about 7500 years BP to perhaps as recently as 2000 to 3000 years BP. The hallmarks of the lithic assemblages of this tradition include large, bifacial side/corner notched and stemmed projectile points, bifacial knives, and large scrapers. Although the mammoth, bison, and horse of the Ice Age had disappeared, these people inhabited the region and exploited its resources (e.g., large terrestrial mammals such as caribou, muskoxen, and moose) in much the same way as their ancient predecessors.

Roughly 5000 years BP, a new cultural entity appeared in arctic Alaska — the Eskimo. While the Eskimo were not among the first residents of arctic Alaska, their more varied and sophisticated technology allowed them to more fully exploit the resources of the region than their Northern Archaic predecessors/neighbors had been able to do. Soon they were dominant and more numerous than any of the groups that had previously inhabited the area. Their technological sophistication enabled them to exploit both the coastal and interior ecosystems and to expand eastward into Canada and Greenland. There is an unbroken record of their use of arctic Alaska since they first appeared in the region (Reanier 1997; Sheehan 1997). The technological signatures of the Eskimo cultures are a chipped stone industry of small, often delicate, well-made bifacial projectile points, ground stone implements, a variety of well-made, often decorated, bone, ivory, and antler tools and items of personal adornment, as well as a propensity for the manufacture of composite tools. At this time pottery appears as well as the use of semi-subterranean houses (Irving 1964; Dumond 1987).

The succession of the Eskimo cultures began with the Denbigh Flint Complex people (ca. 4500 to 2500 years BP), who were followed by the Choris (ca. 2800 to 2200 years BP), Norton (ca. 2400 to 1800 years BP), and Ipiutak (ca. 1900 to 1200 years BP) cultures (Giddings 1964; Giddings and Anderson 1986; Dumond 1987). These closely related, sometimes contemporary, cultural groups together make up what archaeologists generally refer to as the Arctic Small Tool tradition (Irving 1964). These early Eskimos spent as much or more time living in and exploiting the subsistence resources of the foothills and mountains of the Brooks Range as they did the Arctic coast (Kunz 1991; Schoenberg 1995).

About 1,400 years BP, some technological innovations, such as drag floats, caused a switch in emphasis so that there was a bit more exploitation of the maritime resources than previously had been the case. This shift was initiated by the Birnirk people and allowed them to successfully exploit maritime resources, particularly whales, to a greater extent than the earlier Eskimo cultures (Stanford 1976; Giddings and Anderson 1986; Sheehan 1997). This trend continued and reached full flower with the Thule people (ca. 1100 to 500 BP) and on into the historic period (Bockstoce 1976, 1986; Sheehan 1997). At the same time, related but less numerous populations, referred to as Late Prehistoric Eskimos, continued to exploit the resources of the interior, primarily subsisting on caribou and other large terrestrial mammals. They usually overwintered in semi-subterranean houses on the margins of lakes that contained plentiful fish resources (Gerlach and Hall 1988). These people may have been the antecedents of the modern Nunamiut or Inland Eskimo which seem to appear in the archaeological record between 400 and 300 years BP (Kunz and Phippen 1988; Sheehan 1997). The primary difference between the Nunamiut and the preceding Late Prehistoric Eskimos, was that the Nunamiut adopted a strategy of over-wintering in sod houses or caribou skin tents in river valley willow patches.

Contact between the Euro-American arctic whaling fleet and arctic Alaskan Natives first occurred during the mid-19th century. What followed was more than 50 years of continuous contact that drastically altered a traditional culture and set in motion a massive alteration of Native Alaskan lifestyle (Brower 1942; Foote 1964; Bockstoce 1986). In just a few generations, the indigenous people of arctic Alaska moved from the Stone Age to the Atomic Age.

Rarely does a single cultural group hold sway over a region as large as arctic Alaska for such an extended period of time. The modern indigenous population of arctic Alaska is as successful today, subsisting in one of the harshest environments on the planet, as were their ancestors of 5000 years BP. The hard evidence that supports this story, the material culture of arctic Alaska, resides in thousands of prehistoric and historic sites distributed throughout the region. These sites contain the physical manifestation of the culture history of arctic Alaska. This nonrenewable resource must be protected and managed wisely for both its scientific and cultural value.

The Mesa Paleoindians

Archaeologists generally identify cultural entities in the preceramic archaeological record by type and style of flaked stone tools. Most cultural complexes have a distinctive artifact, usually a projectile point, that is diagnostic of that complex, and related complexes usually share a suite of common artifacts. The classic Paleoindian complexes of the North American High Plains and Southwest all share a common suite of tools and manufacturing techniques (Irwin and Wormington 1970; Frison 1978). These Paleoindian complexes are typified by lanceolate shape projectile points which exhibit heavy edge grinding along much of the basal half of the point, excellent workmanship, and stylistic consistency within the individual complexes. Single- and multi-spurred gravers, end scrapers, and distinctive flak-

ing detritus are also hallmarks of these complexes, as is the practice of resharpening broken projectile points in the haft (Irwin and Wormington 1970; Judge 1973; Frison and Stanford 1974; Frison 1988).

Mesa Complex projectile points are lanceolate forms which exhibit all of the traits previously described and are manufactured using the techniques employed by the classic Paleoindian cultures (Figure 9). The suite of tools and type of lithic detritus common to these cultures are also present in the Mesa lithic assemblage in the same ratios as they are in the classic Paleoindian complexes. In addition, the occurrence of in-haft resharpened projectile points is high in the Mesa assemblage (Kunz and Reanier 1995).

The Paleoindian cultures of temperate North America occupied that region between ca. 11,500 and 8500 years BP, and their primary subsistence resources were large Ice Age mammals. In arctic Alaska, the Mesa people were present during the same time period and subsisted on the same types of animals. The weight of these identical technological and cultural elements rule out independent invention/cultural evolution, and there can be no doubt that the Mesa Complex is part of the Paleoindian cultural tradition.

NATURAL SETTING AND SITE DESCRIPTION
Natural Setting

The Mesa Site lies along the northern flank of the Endicott Mountains in the central Brooks Range of arctic Alaska on the east side of the Iteriak Creek valley (Figure 11). The site is surrounded by gently rolling tundra-covered topography that extends northward 40 miles to the Colville River. The floor of the Iteriak Valley is about 2000 feet above sea level. The site lies atop a mesa-like ridge which rises about 180 feet above the valley floor and provides a 360° unobstructed view of approximately 40 square miles. The Mesa, an east-west trending ridge approximately 800 feet long by 300 feet wide, is an erosional remnant of medium-grained gabbro and basalt that was intruded into thinly bedded chert and sili-

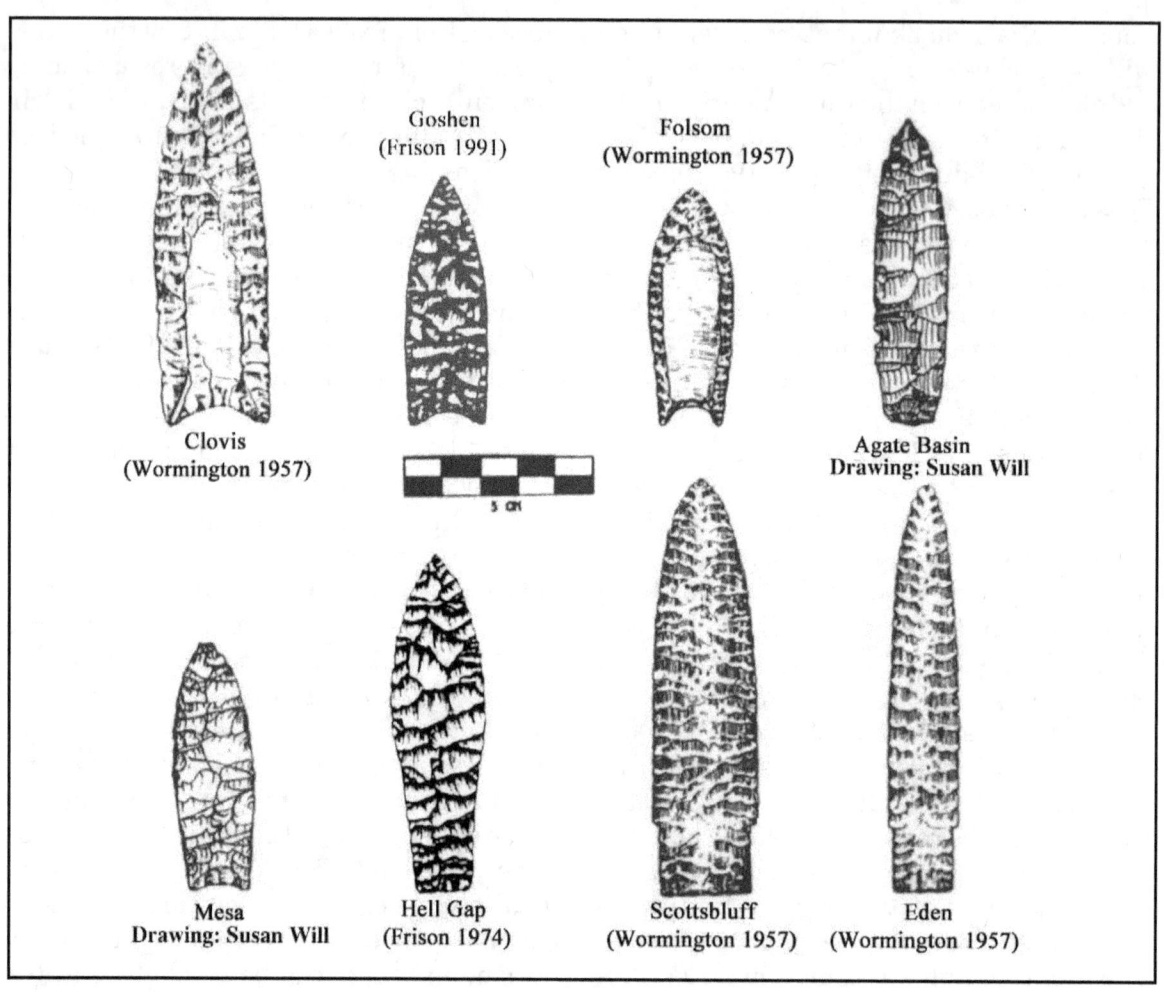

Figure 9. Comparison of classic Paleoindian projectile points and a Mesa projectile point. (After Kunz and Reanier 1995)

ceous shale as part of the mountain building event that formed the Brooks Range about 125 million years ago (C. G. Mull, personal communication 1994) (Figure 10). Local bedrock includes conglomerates, limestones, shales, siltstones, sandstones, cherts and mafic igneous forms (Chapman et al.1964; Beikman and Lathram 1976). The southwestern, western, and northwestern faces of the Mesa are quite sheer, while the other faces are steep, but accessible by walking. The Mesa is flanked by a near continuous talus, which in places almost reaches the summit. The surface of the Mesa is covered by a soil that is the result of aeolian deposition and *in situ* decomposition of bedrock. The soil ranges in depth from two to 14 inches and caps a layer of bedrock rubble that may be up to six feet thick. Isolated tor-like bedrock projections form topographic high points on the eastern and cen-

tral portions of the Mesa.

Much of the Arctic Foothills region has never been glaciated. The last glaciation to occur in the Iteriak Valley was during the early Pleistocene. At the last glacial maximum, ca. 22,000 years BP, glaciers in the region appear to have terminated at the northern front of the Brooks Range, about seven miles south of the Mesa (Hamilton 1986; Mann et al. 2002) (Figure 11). As a result, the Mesa and the Iteriak valley have probably not been covered with glacial ice for at least the last two million years. However, the effects of late Pleistocene glaciation are very apparent on the landscape surrounding the Mesa. The character of the Iteriak valley has been significantly influenced by glacial outwash and other effects of the nearby melting glaciers as well as the dynamics of a peri-glacial environment. In fact, these conditions probably had a lot to

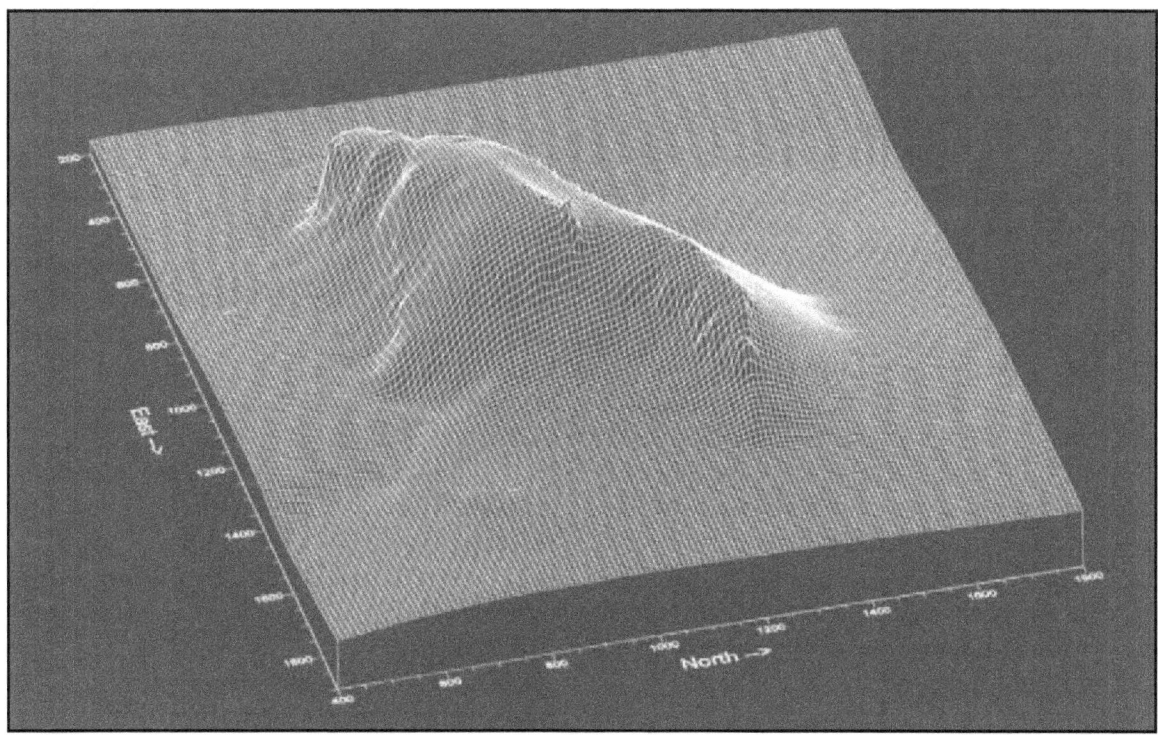

Figure 10. Topographic schematic of the Mesa. (After Durand et al. 1998)

do with the appeal of the Mesa to the late Pleistocene human inhabitants of the area.

Although slightly warmer and wetter now than during the late Pleistocene, the climate along the north flank of the Brooks Range remains cold and dry with a mean annual temperature of -9.6°C (Zhang et al. 1997), and an annual precipitation average of 12.5 inches (Kane et al. 1992). Half of the precipitation is snow, which persists on the ground for eight months of the year (Mann et al. 2002). February is the coldest month, averaging -38.2°C, while July is the warmest, averaging 7.7°C. Rainfall increases during the cyclonic storms of July, August, and September, and reaches a monthly peak in August with an average of 1.9 inches (Reanier 1982; Kane et al. 1992). Most of these storms originate in the Bering Sea and cross the Brooks Range in a northeasterly direction (Moritz 1979). Local surface winds are usually from the northeast or southwest. Winds in excess of 45 miles per hour and of multiple day duration occur occasionally, and wind-free days are rare. Wind is a blessing in the summer as it keeps the mosquitoes at tolerable levels, but during winter it can send wind-chill factors plunging to in-

credible extremes.

While the region is classified as semi-arid by the Thornthwaite method, during the summer months the tundra is quite moist and the soils in many locales are saturated (Patric and Black 1968; Newman and

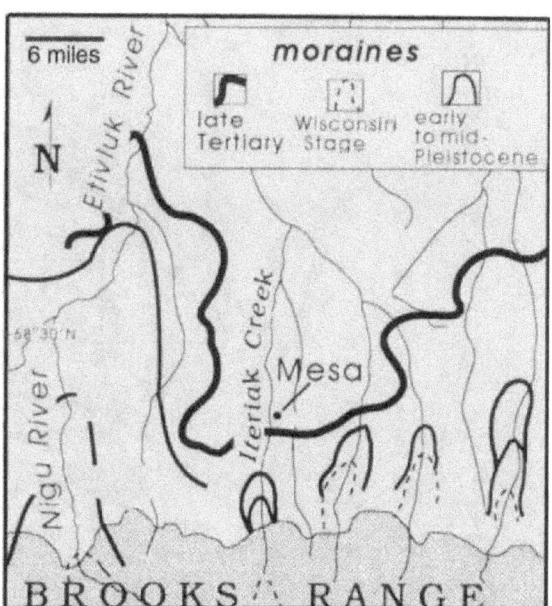

Figure 11. The location of the Mesa in relation to glacial limits of the last 2 million years. (Illustration: Daniel Mann)

9

Branton 1972). Although actual evapotranspiration exceeds annual runoff and potential evapotranspiration exceeds total annual precipitation, soils are often saturated and the surface remains moist because water tables are perched on frozen, ice-rich substrate (Hinzman et al. 1996; Rovansek et al. 1996). Evapotranspiration is greatest in early summer before active layers fully thaw, and precipitation in late summer recharges soil moisture during a period when evapotranspiration is low, therefore the situation is annually persistent (Hinzman et al. 1996; Zhang et al. 1997). This was not the case in the late Pleistocene when precipitation was less and vegetative cover was of a type that allowed more solar radiation (available from more cloud-free days than at present) to keep ice-rich permafrost at a greater depth below surface (Mann et al. 2002).

There are two primary types of tundra that cover most of arctic Alaska: moist acidic tundra which is predominant southward from the northern face of the Arctic Foothills, and non-acidic tundra ranging northward from the foothills across the Coastal Plain (Mann et al. 2001). The Mesa lies within the Arctic Foothills province. Moist acidic tundra (*Sphagno-Eriophoretum*) is dominated by dwarf shrubs (*Betula nana, Ledum palustre, Salix planifoila pluchra*), tussock sedges (*Eriophorum vaginatum*), and acidophilous mosses, among which Sphagnum species are prominent (Mann et al. 2002).

Three plant communities are common on and in the immediate vicinity of the Mesa: cottongrass tussock meadows around the base of the Mesa, flood plain communities adjacent to Mesa and Iteriak creeks, and a dry upland community atop the site (Spetzman 1959). These three plant communities were further divided into six zones to facilitate a vegetation collection and recordation survey, (Watson 1999) (Figure 12).

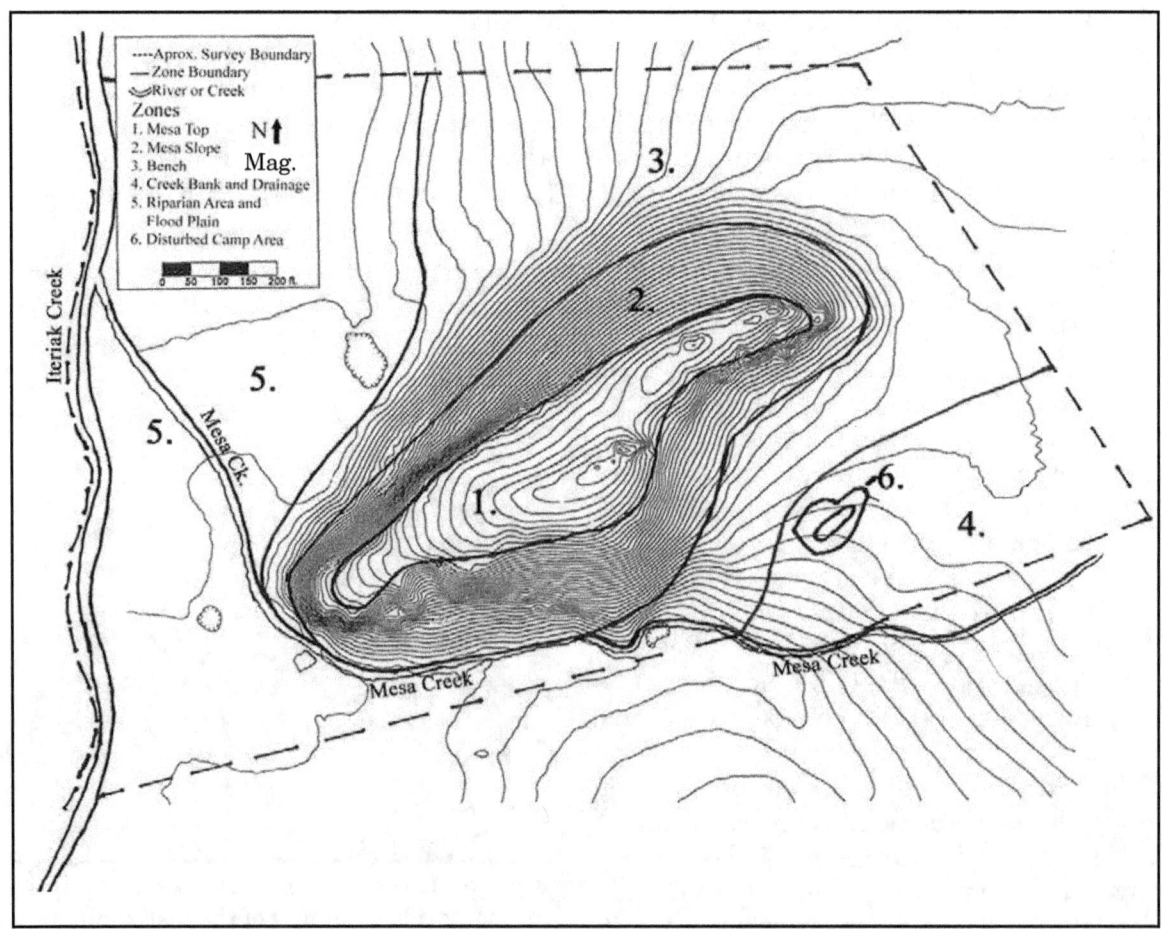

Figure 12. Mesa vegetation zones. (After Durand et al. 1998; Watson 1999)

More specifically, a total of 133 vascular plant taxa representing 71 genera and 30 families; 35 bryophyte taxa (31 mosses and 4 hepatics) representing 24 genera and 17 families; and 36 lichen taxa, representing 22 genera and 13 families were recorded during our investigations at the Mesa (Watson 1999).

Although dominated by cottongrass (*Eriophorum* spp.), the tussock meadows also contain other graminoids, dwarf shrubs, and herbs. Some edible berries are found in this community such as blueberry (*Vaccinium uliginosum*) and cloudberry (*Rubus chamaemorus*). The flood plain community is dominated by willow (*Salix* spp.), some reaching more than seven feet in height and four inches in diameter. This plant community is the primary source for firewood and wood suitable for dwelling and other construction purposes. In early summer, willow leaves can be eaten. Atop the Mesa the vegetation is dry upland tundra composed of lichen, moss, grasses, herbs, and dwarf woody plants and shrubs — cranberry (*Vaccinium vitis-idaea*) and Eskimo potato (*Hedysarum alpinum*) are most often found in this community (Kunz 1982).

In late Pleistocene times, all of these species were present and their abundance was probably similar to that of today, with the exception of cloudberry which was much less abundant (Mann et al. 2002). The limited number and variety of plant species of food value to humans is reflected in the limited use of plants by historic native populations in the region. Hall (1961) states that ethnohistoric and historic data indicate native Brooks Range people's diet consisted of no more than 3% plant material. All of the useful regional plant species that are known to have been utilized by the indigenous human populations of arctic Alaska are found locally around or on the Mesa (Watson 1999).

Game animals in the area today include grizzly bear, caribou, Dall sheep, and moose. Common furbearers are wolf, fox, wolverine, mink, weasel, marmot, and ground squirrel. Water fowl and ptarmigan are present but not numerous. Raptors include peregrine and gyrfalcons, rough-legged hawk, golden eagle, and short-eared owl. During the Pleistocene, mammoth, horse, caribou and bison were known to inhabit the area and muskox may have been present until the recent past (Matheus 1998). Pleistocene predators include those present in the region today as well as a large cat quite similar to the African lion (Matheus 2000). While fish resources are abundant in the region, as they probably were during the late Pleistocene, they are not sufficient of themselves to support a human population as are the salmon runs of the more southerly regions of Alaska. Arctic grayling can be found in all the streams. Arctic char, lake trout, grayling, and burbot can be found in most lakes with a depth greater than eight feet.

Site Description
Surface and natural stratigraphy

The total surface area of the Mesa is approximately 70,000 square feet, of which nearly one half is suitable for human utilization (Durand et al. 1998). The crest of the long axis of the Mesa is level, or slopes gently to the south and north, and ranges from 40 to 20 feet wide. On its southern aspect the surface of the Mesa is thinly vegetated primarily by dryas and other low woody and herbaceous plants, but also by grass, lichen, and moss. Some mineral soil exposures are also present, probably as a result of the prevailing summer winds, which are out of the south or southwest. Lithic artifacts and detritus are visible on, and protruding from, the surface of these exposures. Weathered bedrock spalls up to two inches in diameter are present on, and in the surface of, both the vegetated and unvegetated areas. Along its northern aspect, the Mesa is more robustly vegetated with few mineral soil exposures, and few occurrences of surface cultural material.

The soil column consists of the same basic units site-wide, although some variation is present due to differing soil depths (Reanier 1982). The organic soil horizons range from thin and discontinuous ($<\frac{1}{2}$inch) to a black horizon that may be slightly more than one inch thick. The A1 horizon is well developed in sandy loam, dark brown in color, and may be up to six inches thick. In some parts of the site there is no clearly developed B horizon, while in others there is a dark brown B2ir horizon. C horizons are gravelly and dark yellow in color (Reanier 1982). Underlying this is a layer of bedrock rubble exceeding several feet in thickness and composed of spalls ranging from two to six inches or greater in diameter (Figure 13).

Soil profiles exposed during excavation suggest that over most of the site the soil mantling the bedrock rubble is relatively stable. Wide lateral continuity of individual soil horizons and relatively well developed profiles suggest that disturbance resulting from seasonal freezing and thawing has been minimal, probably because of the excellent drainage provided by the coarse, shattered gabbro substrate. While the generally coarse nature of the soil and lack of moisture appear to have kept frost churning to a minimum over most of the site, excavation has revealed some remnants of ancient frost boils which appear to have developed at some time in the distant past.

Given the site's unique morphology and exposure to the elements, the amount of soil that caps the Mesa is relatively thick when compared with that of other similar geomorphic features in the region. After experiencing many windy days excavating at the site and observing the dynamics of the wind, we suspect that the soil on top of the Mesa is primarily the result of aeolian deposition of materials derived from the talus slopes that ring the site. It appears that aeolian deposition is responsible for the relatively rapid burial of the cultural remains atop the Mesa. This accounts for the excellent preservation of hearth charcoal and the fact that most of the cultural material is buried.

Forty hearths have been exposed by archaeological excavation at the Mesa. In all cases there is undisturbed profile development above the hearths, and the bottoms of the hearths lie on or are slightly within the bedrock rubble. This suggests that the surface upon which the soil developed is older than the site's oldest radiocarbon date of 11,660 years BP. This provides a minimum date for the beginning of soil development/deposition and a basis for a chronologic framework for soil profile development. In profile, the hearth/charcoal deposits suggest they are the remnants of campfires that burned in shallow excavations. Since in most cases hearth excavation extends into the rubble, this suggests that as recently as 11,660 years BP soil thickness at the site was minimal, certainly no more than an inch or so. Although in a few cases the hearth remnants have been distorted by frost-churning or other types of cryoturbation, especially hearths in the more silty sediments, the generally undisturbed nature of the majority of the charcoal deposits testifies to the stability of near-surface stratigraphy over the last 11,660 years. Even in the cases where some frost-churning is evident, there is undisturbed soil profile development above the hearths, suggesting the cryoturbation occurred at some time in the distant past. Additionally, the fact that artifacts and debitage are concentrated around the hearths indicates there has been only minimal lateral disturbance due to cryoturbation and other natural forces.

Localities and cultural stratigraphy

Across the site cultural materials are concentrated in areas that are level or have a gentle slope. Artifacts are generally arranged in distinct clusters, commonly associated with a hearth or hearths. We have subdivided the site into four localities which are defined by topographic features as distinct areas that contain abundant cultural debris (Figure 14). From southwest to northeast, these are Localities "A," "Saddle," "B," and "East Ridge." Excavation has shown that the distribution of surface artifacts, particularly in Locality A, indicates that these localities reflect true concentrations of cultural detritus, and are not simply a function of excavation exposure. Although this circumstance cannot be demonstrated in Locality Saddle, where artifacts are generally not visible on the surface and cultural deposits are deeper, excavation has revealed

Mesa Site Soil Profile Descriptions

Site Description	Horizon	Depth cm	Color (Moist)	Texture	Structure	Consistence	Roots	Boundary
PROFILE 1 **CLASSIFICATION:** Pergelic Cryorthent fragmental, mixed, frigid **ALTITUDE:** 700m **PARENT MATERIAL:** Colluvium derived from gabbro **VEGETATION:** Sparse Dryas octopetala, grasses, saxifrage, Cladonia sp. and other lichens **SLOPE AND ASPECT:** 3° South **TEMPERATURE:** Air (+1 meter) 10°C, surface 13°C, 25cm 9°C, 50 cm 7°C July 9, 1980, 1300.	01 02 A1 C1 C2	0-10 10-35 35-50+	Discontinuous sparse litter of *Dryas* leaves and grass Discontinuous thin layer of decomposed organic material 7.5YE 2.5/2 10YR 3/4 10YR 3/4	gsl vgl g	2fsbk*mcr 1fcr —	fr,ss,sp fr,ss,sp —	2vf&f 2vf&f 1vf&f	as cs
PROFILE 2 **CLASSIFICATION:** Pergelic Cryochrept, fragmental, mixed, frigid. **ALTITUDE:** 700m **PARENT MATERIAL:** Colluvium derived from gabbro **VEGETATION:** *Dryas octopetala, Vaccinium uliginosum*, grasses, *Cassiope tetragona*, sparse lichens. **SLOPE AND ASPECT:** 4° S20°W **TEMPERATURES:** Air (+ 1meter) 14°C, Surface 14°C, 10 cm 11°C 25 cm 11°C, 35 cm 8°C July 10, 1980, 1200	01 02 A1 B2ir IIC1 IIIC2 (frost heave intrusion)	0.5-0 1-0 0-7 7-14 14-35+ 12-35+	Discontinuous layer of Dryas leaves and grass Discontinuous layer of decomposed organic material 7.5YR 3/2 7.5YR 4/4 10YR 4/3 10YR 4/3	sl l g gsl	2fsbk*fcr 1vfcr — 2fsbk	fr,ss,sp fr,ss,sp — fi,ss,sp	2vf&f 2vf&f 1vf 1vf	aw aw

NOTE: The bottom surfaces of all stones in these profiles are coated with a reddish black (10YR 2/1, moist) stain. Some of the larger stones also have slight carbonate deposits.

Abbreviations:
Texture: v-very; s-sandy; g-gravel; gravelly; l-loam.
Structure: 1-weak; 2-moderate; vf-very fine; f-fine; m-medium; sbk-subangular blocky; cr-crumb;* -breaking to.
Consistence: fr-moist, friable; fi-moist, firm; ss-wet, slighty sticky; sp-wet, slightly plastic.
Roots: 1-few; 2-common; vf-very fine; f-fine.
Boundary: a-abrupt; c-clear; s-smooth; w-wavy.

Figure 13. After Reanier 1982.

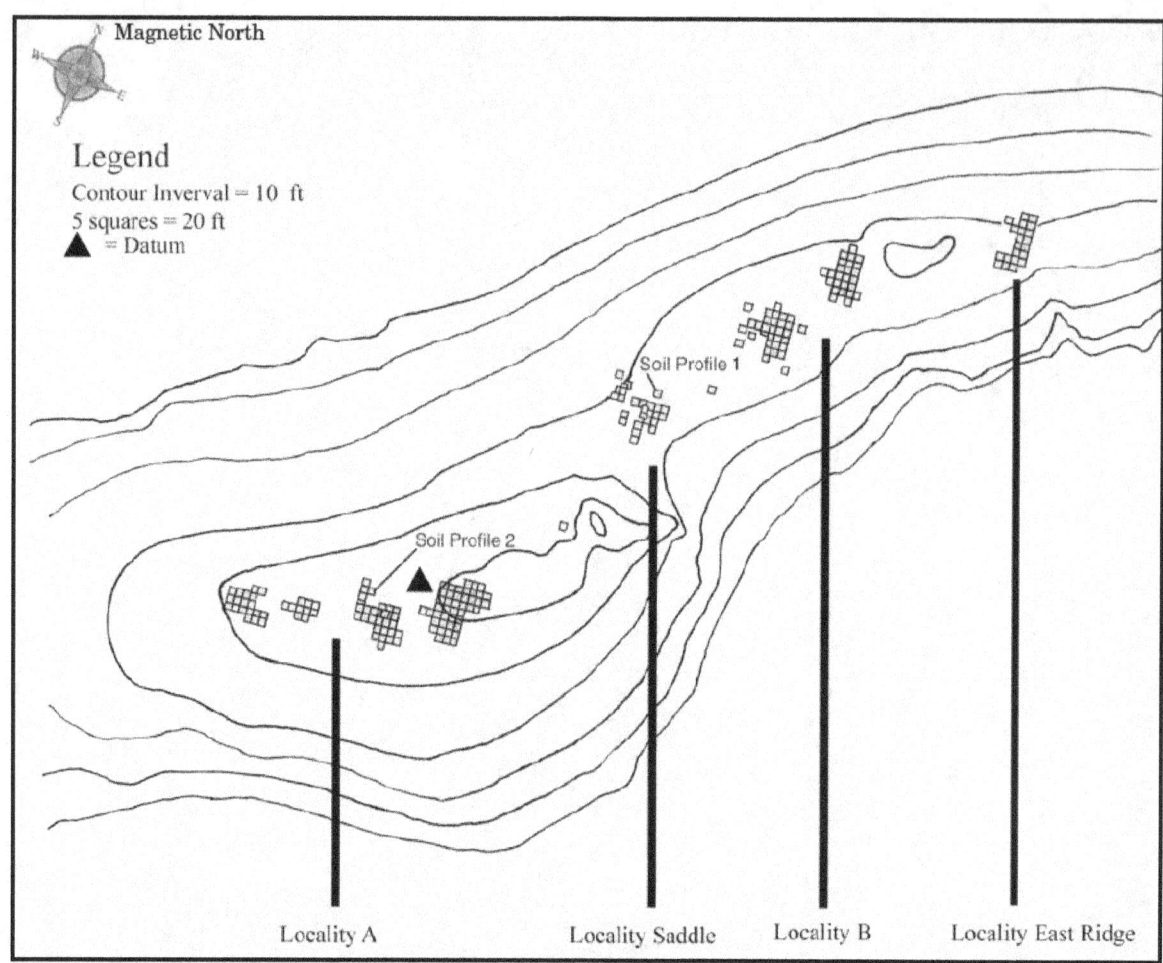

Figure 14. Mesa excavation localities and soil profile locations.

artifact distribution patterns identical to those in the other localities of the site.

Locality A lies on the most elevated portion of the site and encompasses all of the reasonably level ground on the south side of the Mesa's median crest. Southward from the level crest area the surface slopes downward with rapidly increasing steepness. In its western quadrant, the surface of Locality A slopes to the west as well as the south. At more than 14,000 square feet this is the largest locality at the site. Thin vegetation covers a shallow soil that rarely exceeds four inches in depth. Most of the surface artifacts found at the site were collected from this locality. However, most of the cultural material in Locality A was buried and numerous artifacts and thousands of waste flakes, as well as a number of hearths, have been revealed through the excavation of 100.5 grid squares in four distinct activity/use areas. The total excavated area in Locality A is 1608 square feet.

Locality Saddle lies between localities A and B, and encompasses an area of approximately 8000 square feet. Much of this locality lies in a shallow basin containing soil up to 14 inches thick. The most deeply buried cultural material at the site occurs in this locality. Numerous artifacts and flakes were recovered from the bedrock rubble up to two feet below surface. Locality Saddle supports the site's most robust vegetation mat. The only area of erosion in this locality occurs in the southeastern portion where there is some headward encroachment of an area of aeolian scouring at the break in slope. Artifacts and waste flakes have been observed eroding out of the soil/vegetation mat at the erosional contact. A total of 23.5 grid squares have been excavated in this locality, yielding numerous artifacts, thousands of flakes, and a number of hearths. The excavated area amounts to 376 square feet.

Locality B lies in the northeastern portion of the site about 20 feet lower and about 100 feet northeast of Locality A. The total area encompassed by this locality approaches 10,000 square feet. The initial site excavation conducted in 1979 occurred on a slight rise in the central portion of this locality. The vegetation cover is generally robust, which is probably the reason for the low occurrence of surface artifacts. Soil depth varies, ranging from two to ten inches. In most cases soil depth appears to reflect subsurface bedrock topography. A total of 56.5 grid squares, totaling 904 square feet have been excavated in two distinct activity/use areas, producing numerous artifacts and thousands of flakes, as well as a large number of hearths. The oldest date for the site, 11,660 years BP, comes from a hearth in this locality.

As its name suggests, the East Ridge Locality is the easternmost excavation area. Situated in a small saddle between two bedrock outcrops, this locality encompasses an area of roughly 600 square feet. The locality is moderately vegetated, and displayed a light scattering of cultural material on the surface. Soil depth ranges from three to nine inches, and is deepest along the central eastern boundary. A single block of 21 grid squares, or 336 square feet, produced numerous artifacts, thousands of waste flakes, and several hearths. Unlike other Mesa hearths, one of the East Ridge hearths had two flat stone slabs associated with it, as well as several scrapers. Additionally, the charcoal/soil matrix of this hearth contained burned bone as well as a variety of flakes and artifacts.

Thirteen seasons of field work at the Mesa have demonstrated that the lithic artifacts and debitage are culturally homogeneous from the surface to the bedrock rubble, and that the site can be viewed as possessing a single cultural component, excepting a highly localized intrusive element in Locality A, which will be discussed later. Accordingly, the site has been excavated, and flakes and artifacts collected by recognizable natural units: "surface," which is the vegetated or unvegetated surface of the ground; "root mat," which includes the subsurface vegetation and organic soil; "subsurface," which includes all mineral soil horizons; and "rubble," which refers to the zone of shattered bedrock that underlies the soil. Excavation has demonstrated on average, that less than five percent of a given square's cultural material will be recovered from the surface, 10 to 15 per cent will be recovered from the root mat, 70 to 90 per cent will be recovered from the subsurface, and less than five per cent recovered from the rubble. The sole exception occurs in Locality Saddle, where a substantial amount of cultural material was recovered well into the rubble level. Along with most of the flakes and artifacts, the hearths are found in the subsurface level, usually resting on or in the upper portion of the rubble level. These data suggest there is probably only one zone of occupation, the subsurface level, and that the cultural material recovered from the levels above and below, is present there as the result of depositional and post-depositional dynamics, such as trampling, and seasonal freezing and thawing.

Cultural features

The only cultural features encountered at the Mesa are hearths (N=40), the remains of ancient campfires (Figure 15). Compared with other sites of great antiquity and somewhat similar settings in the region, the degree of hearth preservation at the Mesa is unusual. As previously mentioned, the amount of soil, and the well developed soil profiles overlying the hearths, suggest that the number of hearths and their excellent preservation result from relatively rapid burial following the use events.

In cross section most of the hearths are roughly lenticular and rarely exceed five inches in thickness (Figure 16). They are unlined, and many of the hearths appear to lie in shallow depressions excavated into the shattered bedrock rubble. In generalized plan-view, the hearths are characterized by an irregular shaped core of very dark charcoal-rich soil, which generally does not exceed eight inches in diameter or linear extent. The charcoal-rich core, which contains chunks and flecks of charcoal along with artifacts and waste flakes, is irregularly

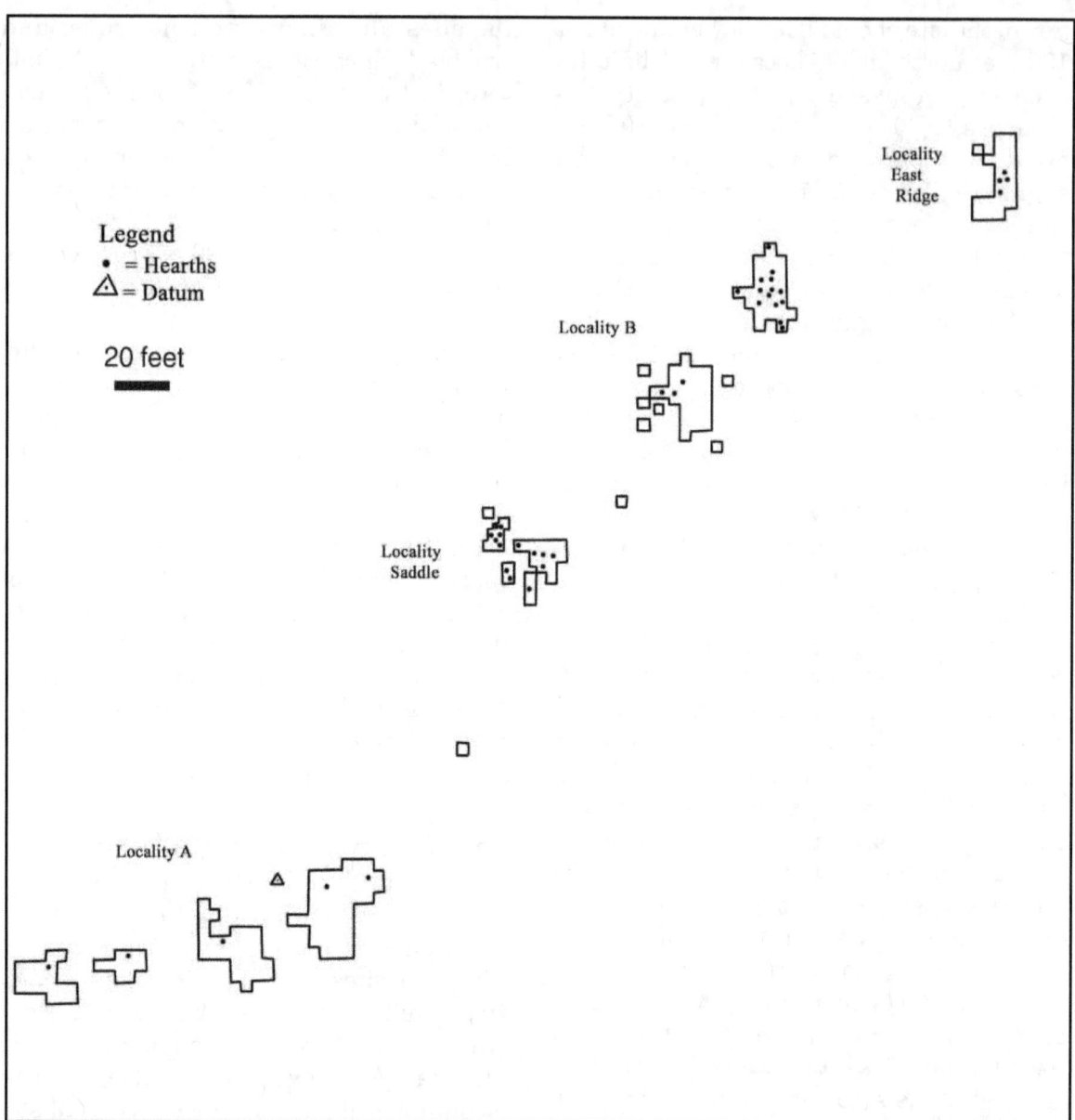

Figure 15. Location of hearths on the Mesa.

surrounded by an oxidized reddish soil which contains charcoal flecks and cultural material. The oxidized soil extends outward from the core margin three to six inches.

Because of their small size and ephemeral nature, each hearth probably represents a single episode of use. There is no evidence to suggest that multiple hearths (use events) have been superimposed over each other. With the exception of a few of the hearths in Locality B, and the westernmost excavation block in Locality Saddle (areas of deeper sediment), the hearths show few signs of disturbance. Some pieces of charcoal recovered from the

hearths approach one-half inch in diameter, large enough that a portion of their cross section is recognizable, permitting diameter size estimates to be made based on annual-ring curvature. These data suggest the woody taxa burned as fuel by the site's occupants were the same size as most of that growing in the vicinity of the Mesa today. Preliminary analysis of the hearth charcoal suggests that the species used as fuel more than 10,000 years ago are the same as are available in the region today: willow, poplar, and alder (Reanier 1997).

All of the hearths excavated at the site are basically the same in terms of context

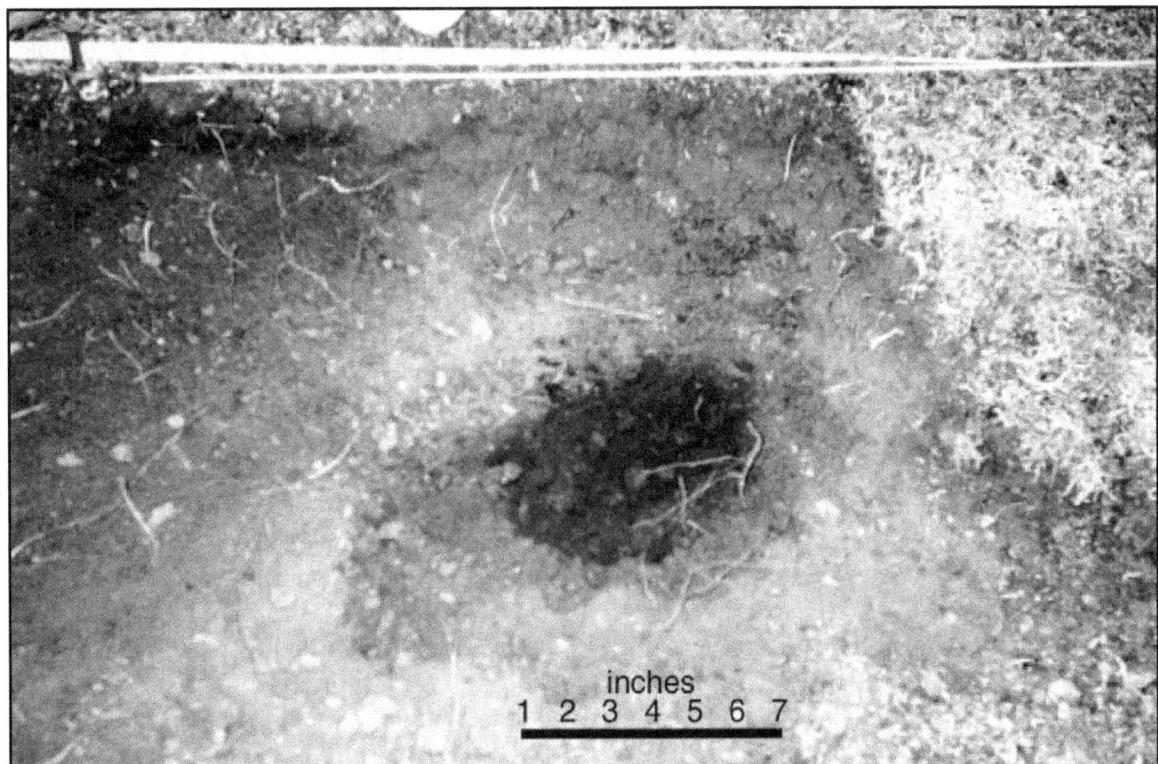

Figure 16. Appearance of typical hearth. (Photo: C. E. Adkins)

and associated materials except for one of the four hearths in the East Ridge Locality. While its matrix contained cultural material similar to that contained in the fill of other hearths, it also contained numerous small pieces of burned bone, most less than one inch in diameter, and several large scrapers. In addition, there were two large, flat slabs of limestone immediately adjacent to the hearth. All this suggests that food preparation may have taken place there. Occasionally the fill of other hearths have produced a few very small pieces of burned bone within the matrix, but not enough to suggest that food preparation had been a primary activity. Charcoal from this hearth dated at ca. 10,000 years BP, the same as most of the other hearths at the site.

EXCAVATION AND COLLECTION METHODOLOGY

In 1978 and 1979 our BLM crew was involved in the excavation of the Lisburne site, about five miles down Iteriak Creek from the Mesa. At the same time, we were also responsible for examining all of the areas in the National Petroleum Reserve-Alaska

(NPR-A) that were slated for possible impact from oil and gas exploration activities. As a result, we had a very limited amount of time to work at the Mesa. Late in the summer of 1978, as a first step in developing a plan for excavating the Mesa, we established a permanent site datum, made a topographic map of the site surface using a plane table and alidade, and plotted the location of all the surface artifacts and significant flakes scatters. Most of the surface cultural material occurred on the south slope, where the vegetation cover was thin and some mineral soil exposures were present. To determine if there was buried cultural material at the site, we undertook test excavations over a two-day period late in the 1979 season. In an area of the site that displayed little surface cultural material, was heavily vegetated, and had reasonable soil depth (later designated Locality B), excavation revealed the presence of subsurface artifacts, detritus, and hearth features, which appeared to be in an undisturbed context. Test excavation in the areas where there were surface flake scatters demonstrated that even in these shallower soils, undisturbed, buried cultural deposits were present. The three original localities, A, Saddle, and B, were tested, and we chose areas for excavation based upon the results of this testing program.

These initial excavations indicated that the site was considerably larger in area than we had presumed, and that the *in situ* cultural deposits had the potential to add a tremendous amount of significant data to the arctic Alaska archaeological record. Therefore, in 1980 we spent about ten days at the site engaged in an extensive testing program. This work demonstrated that large areas of the site contained extensive deposits of buried cultural material, and at the same time provided initial insights into the natural and cultural stratigraphy. The testing effort also suggested that there was only one cultural component at the site.

We established a site grid system based on magnetic compass bearings. The grid utilized the English measurement system, and the standard excavation units were four feet square. Initially, excavation was done in arbitrary two inch levels. However, as it became evident that the site was comprised of a single cultural component, we began to excavate according to the naturally occurring stratigraphic units in the geologic profile. Not being constrained to arbitrary levels allowed excavation to more closely reflect the effects of the soil formation process and dynamics on the cultural deposits. The vertical provenience of all artifacts was determined by their depth below the surface of the excavation unit, while horizontal provenience was measured by the distance from datum. All excavation units (squares) were subdivided into four quadrants designated northwest, northeast, southwest, and southeast.

The squares were hand troweled by level, with each quadrant in a level being excavated and the recovered cultural material bagged individually. Each level was mapped separately. All squares contained a surface, root mat, and subsurface level, but not all contained a rubble level. The back-dirt from each individual quadrant was screened separately through a one-quarter inch mesh screen and cultural material was bagged

apart from the *in situ* material. Beginning in 1994, we also screened the material that passed through the one-quarter inch screen through a one-eighth inch mesh. Material from the one-quarter inch mesh was bagged separately from that recovered from the one-eighth inch screen. Formal and incidental tools, as well as retouched flakes, were bagged individually, while waste flakes were bagged as "flake lots." Thus, each quadrant (with the possible exception of quadrants in the surface level) could have artifact and flake lot envelopes that reflected *in situ*, as well as one-quarter inch, and one-eighth inch screen recovery[3].

The excavation of each square was recorded in the field using *"Rite in the Rain"* No. 351 Field Notebooks. The surface condition, including topography, amount and type of vegetation, disturbance, slope, and aspect of each square was recorded prior to excavation. A map of each excavation level was accompanied by a physical description of the level and its contents, as well as the observations of the excavator(s). Artifacts were mapped in with exact provenience while flake locations were recorded using the approximating 'eyeball' method. Artifact and flake-lot envelopes were labeled with the site designation, locality designation, square provenience, level, quadrant, recovery method, specific provenience (if the material recovered was a tool, other type of formal artifact, or hearth fill), the date, and the excavator's name. Upon completing the excavation of a square, all material collected from that square was placed in a similarly labeled container(s) with the additional notation that therein was all the material recovered from that particular square.

With the exception of large chunks of charcoal encountered while excavating, most hearth fill was collected as a bulk sample after the hearth feature was mapped and troweled. Charcoal, as well as other cultural material, was extracted from the hearth fill in the laboratory. Hearth fill was

---

3 We considered anything that was loose on the surface to be part of the surface level. On well vegetated squares there was usually a considerable amount of loose organic debris. This material would often be collected by dragging a trowel across the surface and subsequently screened.

passed successively through one-quarter, one-eighth, and one-sixteenth inch mesh sieves and the charcoal as well as other cultural material was removed by hand picking under magnification. Artifacts, flakes, and other collected material were cataloged in the laboratory after our return from the field. In most cases, tools and flakes were not cleaned so that possible cultural residues would not be compromised.

CHRONOLOGY

Fifty-one radiocarbon dates have been produced by 28 of the 40 hearths excavated at the Mesa (Figure 17). Forty-four of the dates are AMS and seven are standard radiometric assays. Dense concentrations of flakes in and around the hearths, as well as burned diagnostic artifacts within the hearth matrix, demonstrate the strong association between dated hearths and related artifact clusters.

The first Mesa radiocarbon date of 7,620 ± 95 years BP (DIC-1589)[4], has been discarded. This decision was based on an AMS date of 10,060 years BP obtained from an archived portion of the original sample, as well as dates from other hearths at the site, all of which exceeded the original date by at least 2000 years. The other standard radiometric dates from the site have also been removed from the general chronology as they were obtained for a study which compares the variation in results of standard and AMS radiocarbon dates. This study has important ramifications in terms of dating any site of late Pleistocene age. It also points out the inadvisability of mixing the results of AMS and standard radiocarbon dates from this time period. Therefore, standard radiometric dates are not being used in the development of the Mesa's chronology (Kunz 1998).

All but three of the 44 AMS dates cluster between 10,300 and 9700 years BP. One of the three outlier dates, 9330 ± 40 years BP (Beta-125996) is believed to have been contaminated when it was collected, and is rejected because a second assay of charcoal

from that hearth returned a date of 9780 ± 40 years BP (Beta-130577). The other two outlier dates, 11,660 ± 80 years BP (Beta-55286) and 11,190 ± 70 years BP (Beta-57430), can not be rejected and will be discussed later.

The range of dates from the Mesa fall into a problematic period for calibration. There is evidence that the rapid climatic shifts of the Younger Dryas period, ca 11,000 to 10,000 years BP, caused fluctuations in the level of atmospheric C-14 (Bjorck et al. 1996; Hajdas et al. 1998; Kitagawa and van der Plicht 1998; Goslar et al. 2000). As a result, a single radiocarbon date from this period could in fact cover a span of more than 500 years. This has been demonstrated by the work of Kitagawa and van der Plicht (1998) at Lake Sigetsu, Japan. The lake's annual varves (sediment layers) were radiocarbon dated, producing a curve where multiple C-14 dates can refer to the same point in time (Figure 18). A corroborative example of this circumstance comes from the Mesa, where 13 radiocarbon samples from a single hearth were assayed and returned dates that ranged from 10,260 ± 110 years BP (Beta-96070) to 9850 ± 150 years BP (Beta-96067), a range of more than 400 years (Mann et al. 2001). These dates span nearly the full range of the rest of the dates for Mesa (excepting the outliers), and since the samples come from one hearth, in all probability, they reflect a single brief use episode. These circumstances make it not only impossible to temporally separate phases of occupation, but also make it impossible to tightly constrain the period of overall occupation.

The remaining two outlier dates, 11,190 ± 70 years BP and 11,660 ± 80 years BP, clearly lie outside of the range of the other dates. Both of these AMS dates were derived from multiple distinct pieces of charcoal collected from the same hearth matrix, which in appearance was no different than any of the other hearths encountered at Mesa. Numerous flakes and artifacts were associated with this hearth, and a classic Mesa projectile point was recovered from the hearth fill. The field notes indicate that the hearth was excavated and materials collected in the standard manner, and that no anomalies or

---

[4] All Mesa radiocarbon dates, standard and AMS, are reported in radiocarbon years before 1950.

MESA RADIOCARBON DATES

Date Reported	Laboratory Sample Number	Location in Excavation Grid	Site Locality	Type of Date	Conventional Radiocarbon Age
1980	DIC-1589	N179-183/E146-150 N175-179/E138-142 N175-179/E142-146	B	Standard	7620 +/- 95 BP
7/13/90	Beta-36805	N117-121/E96-100	Saddle	AMS	9730 +/- 80 BP
1/22/92	Beta-50429	N103-107/E94-98	Saddle	Standard	10980 +/- 280 BP
5/22/92	Beta-50430	N103-107/E94-98	Saddle	AMS	9945 +/- 75 BP
5/22/92	Beta-50428	S1-5/E16-20	A	AMS	10090 +/- 85 BP
7/1/92	Beta-52606	N179-183/E146-150	B	AMS	10060 +/- 70 BP
9/21/92	Beta-55286	N217-219/E180-182	B	AMS	11660 +/- 80 BP
9/21/92	Beta-55285	N217-219/E176-178	B	AMS	10000 +/- 80 BP
9/21/92	Beta-55284	N213-215/E180-182	B	AMS	9930 +/- 80 BP
9/21/92	Beta-55283	N209-211/E184-186	B	AMS	10240 +/- 80 BP
9/21/92	Beta-55282	N109-111/E88-90	Saddle	AMS	9990 +/- 80 BP
11/25/92	Beta-57430	N217-218/E180-181	B	AMS	11190 +/- 70 BP
11/25/92	Beta-57429	N209-211/E176-178	B	AMS	9900 +/- 70 BP
2/11/94	Beta-69900	N211-215/E182-186	B	AMS	10050 +/- 90 BP
2/11/94	Beta-69899	N211-215/E174-178	B	AMS	9900 +/- 80 BP
2/11/94	Beta-69898	N111-115/E98-102	Saddle	AMS	10070 +/- 60 BP
9/11/95	Beta-84650	S23-24/W21-22	A	AMS	10080 +/- 50 BP
9/11/95	Beta-84649	N230-231/E178-179	B	AMS	9980 +/- 60 BP
8/7/96	Beta-95600	N1-N3/E34-36	A	AMS	10230 +/- 60 BP
10/9/96	Beta-96070	N1-N3/E34-36	A	AMS	10260 +/- 110 BP
10/9/96	Beta-96069	S1-N1/E34-36	A	AMS	10150 +/- 130 BP
10/9/96	Beta-96068	S1-N1/E34-36	A	AMS	10080 +/- 120 BP
10/9/96	Beta-96067	S1-N1/E34-36	A	AMS	9850 +/- 150 BP
10/9/96	Beta-96066	S1-N1/E34-36	A	AMS	10090 +/- 110 BP
10/9/96	Beta-96065	S1-N1/E34-36	A	AMS	9810 +/- 110 BP
10/14/96	Beta-95914	S31-33/W86-88	A	AMS	10130 +/- 60 BP
10/14/96	Beta-95913	S27-29/W56-58	A	AMS	10080 +/- 60 BP
7/27/98	Beta-118585	S1-N1/E34-36	A	AMS	10130 +/- 50 BP

Figure 17. (continued next page).

MESA RADIOCARBON DATES

Date Reported	Laboratory Sample Number	Location in Excavation Grid	Site Locality	Type of Date	Conventional Radiocarbon Age
7/27/98	Beta-118584	S1-N1/E34-36	A	AMS	10040 +/- 50 BP
7/27/98	Beta-118583	N1-3/E34-36	A	AMS	10050 +/- 50 BP
7/27/98	Beta-118582	N1-3/E34-36	A	AMS	10100 +/- 50 BP
7/27/98	Beta-118581	N1-N3/E34-36	A	AMS	10170 +/- 50 BP
7/16/98	Beta-119100	N1-3/E34-36	A	AMS	10000 +/- 50 BP
8/31/98	Beta-120400	N253-255/E268-270	East Ridge	AMS	9740 +/- 50 BP
8/31/98	Beta-120399	N125-129/E84-86	Saddle	AMS	9860 +/- 50 BP
8/31/98	Beta-120398	N123-125/E82-84	Saddle	AMS	9920 +/- 50 BP
9/11/98	Beta-120793	N117-119/E100-102	Saddle	AMS	9800 +/- 60 BP
9/16/98	Beta-120397	N251-255/E268-270	East Ridge	Standard	8820 +/- 230 BP
2/1/99	Beta-125998	N255-257/E268-271	East Ridge	AMS	10030 +/- 40 BP
2/1/99	Beta-125997	N255-257/E266-268	East Ridge	AMS	10080 +/- 40 BP
2/1/99	Beta-125996	N253-255/E266-268	East Ridge	AMS	9330 +/- 40 BP
2/1/99	Beta-125995	S1-N1/E34-36	A	Standard	9160 +/- 140 BP
6/17/99	Beta-130577	N251-253/E266-268	East Ridge	AMS	9780 +/- 40 BP
9/18/99	Beta-133354	N121-123/E90-92	Saddle	AMS	9950 +/- 60 BP
9/18/99	Beta-133353	N111-113/E86-88	Saddle	AMS	10180 +/- 60 BP
2/29/00	GX-26461	N255-257/E266-268	East Ridge	Standard	12240 +/- 610 BP
4/19/00	Beta-140199	S31-33/W86-88	A	Standard	9500 +/- 190 BP
4/27/00	GX-26567-AMS	N255-257/E266-268	East Ridge	AMS	9930 +/- 40 BP
4/27/00	Beta-140198	N121-123/E90-92	Saddle	Standard	9480 +/- 710 BP
5/18/00	Beta-142262	S29-33/W84-88	A	AMS	10120 +/- 50 BP
5/18/00	Beta-142261	N121-123/E90-92	Saddle	AMS	10080 +/- 50 BP

All dates are radiocarbon years before 1950
Dates printed in black are AMS
Dates printed in red are Standard Radiometric Dates

Figure 17 (continued).

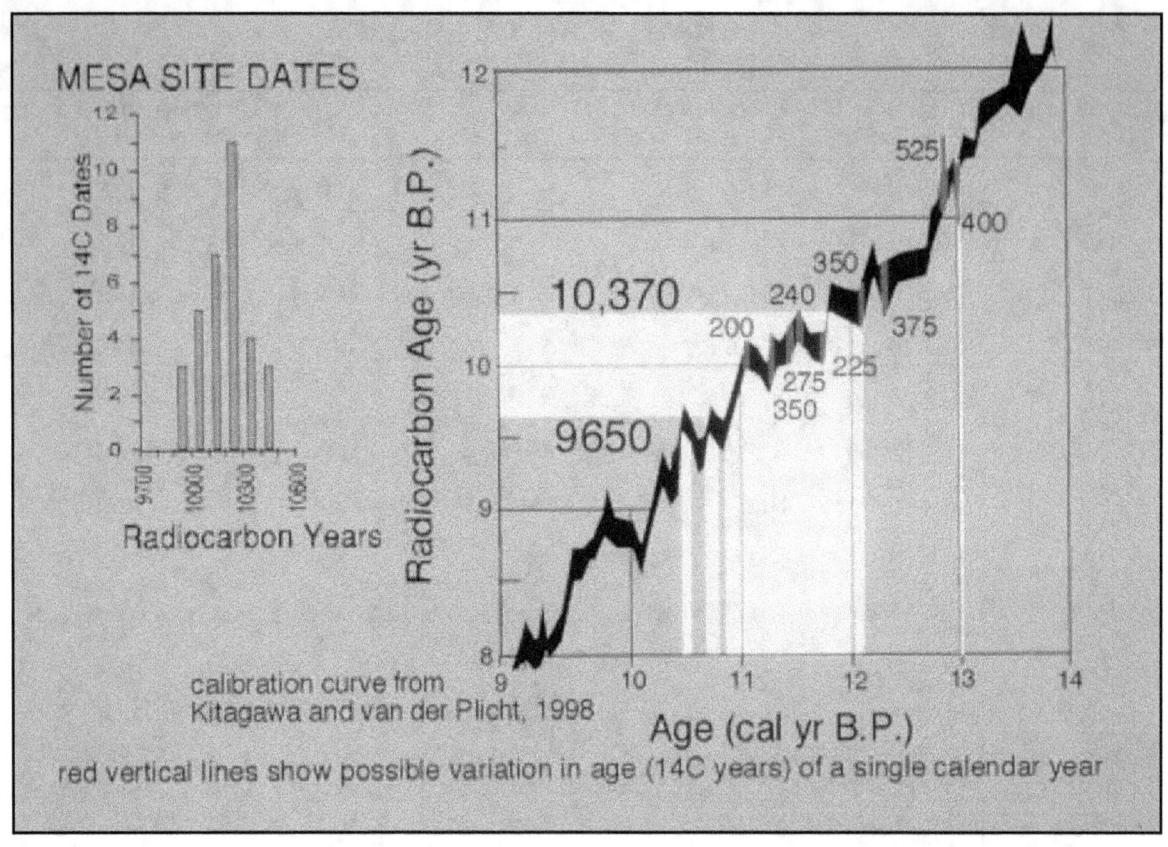

Figure 18. Variability in radiocarbon ages during the Younger Dryas. (Illustration: Daniel Mann)

problems were encountered. No procedural problems were reported from the radiocarbon laboratory.

Several possibilities could account for these older dates. The most straightforward interpretation accepts the dates as accurate. As such, they would provide evidence of occupation of the Mesa at least a thousand years earlier than the other site dates indicate. This interpretation has important ramifications for the position of the Mesa Complex in the late Pleistocene prehistory of North America. It suggests that the Mesa Complex could be as old or older than Clovis, and that the oldest date for the assemblage precedes unfluted Paleoindian materials from the High Plains by at least a thousand years.

It is also possible these older dates might be the result of contamination by ancient carbon. While coal is found across the North Slope, there is no source of contamination on or near the site itself, and the other dates from the site are unaffected.

Another possibility, although unlikely for

the reasons pointed out by Kunz and Reanier (1995), is that the dates could be the result of burning old wood. In the terminal Pleistocene as today, there were three types of wood in the region that were substantial enough to produce an enduring fire: willow, poplar, and alder. None of these lasts in useable form for very long on the surface after it is dead, certainly no longer than 100 years. Yet in the Arctic, it is possible for wood to be incorporated into a frozen matrix, preserved for many thousands of years, and then exposed on the surface once again. However, the circumstances of burial and subsequent thawing almost always render the wood unusable and unattractive for use as fuel. Additionally, the circumstances in which ancient wood might be buried, and subsequently exposed and thawed on the surface, do not occur within close proximity to the Mesa.

While the two 11,000 year old dates are separated by more than 400 years, the separation can be explained by the Younger Dryas effect. The radiocarbon curve of

Kitagawa and van der Plicht (1998) shows that radiocarbon dates of 11,600 years BP and 11,200 years BP could represent a single date at any point within that time span, and could well be the same date. As mentioned previously, this same phenomenon has been noted elsewhere on the site, where multiple dates from the same hearth are divergent by several hundred years.

There is also the possibility that the temporal divergence between these two dates results from the hearth being affected by natural agents. A portion of the hearth was strung out along the linear alignment of a frost crack. In the northeast quadrant of the square just to the west is another hearth, dating to 10,000 +/-80 (Beta-55285) years BP. The field notes indicate that portions of the two hearths are in close proximity. The divergence of the two 11,000 BP dates could reflect the mixing of 10,000 BP charcoal and the older charcoal as a result of cryoturbation and/or excavation and collection .

Another, possibility for contamination is by charcoal from a natural fire. This seems unlikely given the reasons cited by Kunz and Reanier (1995); namely, there is no surface vegetation on the Mesa capable of sustaining a long-lasting fire, nor is the vegetation growing there of the size (diameter) indicated by the charcoal recovered from the hearths. The firewood burned on the Mesa was probably collected from the riparian zone along nearby Iteriak Creek, where willow diameters can exceed three inches.

In support of the validity of these older dates, is the recent work done by Jeff Rasic at Tuluaq Hill in the Noatak drainage (Rasic 2000). At Tuluaq Hill, bifaces very similar to some found at the Mesa were recovered in chronologic contexts of 11,200 years BP.

In any case, these 11,000 BP dates have not been repeated elsewhere on the Mesa, and the fact that 41 of the remaining 43 dates cluster between 9,730 ± 80 and 10,260 ±110 years BP, suggests that an age centered around 10,000 years BP accurately dates the primary period of Mesa occupation. If the assemblage reflects multiple occupations, based on the cluster of 41 dates, the primary use of the site lasted for a period of roughly 400-800 years.

HISTORY OF FIELD WORK AND EXCAVATION

Excavation of the Mesa was conducted over a period of 22 years. Because of the length of this research and the events that occurred during that time period, the following time line is presented so that the reader can develop a perspective relative to the flow and progress of the research.

The Mesa site was discovered in 1978 by Michael Kunz and Dale Slaughter, while conducting archaeological survey as part of an environmental compliance program undertaken by the Bureau of Land Management in the NPR-A (Kunz 1982). The discovery was made during a reconnaissance of a hardrock material source that was proposed for use in the construction of a nearby well-site and airstrip. The Mesa was one of the few igneous (hardrock) outcrops in the area. Examination of the Mesa's surface, revealed lithic debitage, a few complete and fragmentary projectile points, and other stone tools in surface scatters primarily in the south central portion of the site. Although the projectile points appeared to possess classic Paleoindian traits, the total absence of High Plains Paleoindian assemblages in the Arctic caused the site to initially be evaluated as a multi-component surface manifestation that included a few artifacts that were fortuitously Paleoindian-like. Subsequent investigations that summer revealed the site was much larger than originally estimated, and that there was a possibility that it contained buried cultural material. Although we didn't excavate that year, we did make a plane table topographic map of the site, plotted the location of the surface artifacts, and collected the artifacts (Kunz 1982).

In 1979 we conducted a limited two-day test excavation at the site. We designated three localities based on topography and the presence of surface debitage, and established a site grid utilizing four-foot square excavation units. To determine the presence of subsurface cultural material, we conducted the primary testing effort in Locality B. This area was robustly vegetated, appeared to have reasonable soil depth, and displayed little surface indication of cultural material. A total of 12.5 grid squares were excavated; 10.5 in Locality B, one in Locality Saddle, and one in Locality A. Due to time constraints, these excavations were initially conducted using the skim-shovel/screening method. In Locality B we quickly encountered significant flake and artifact concentrations and abandoned the skim-shovel technique in favor of the slower, but more precise hand-troweling method. The excavations in localities Saddle and A also produced subsurface cultural material. This work suggested that most of the cultural material at the site was buried, that the artifact context appeared to be reasonably undisturbed by postdepositional activity, and that some of the stone tools were in direct association with hearths. Thirteen complete and fragmentary projectile points, some biface fragments, flake tools, and numerous waste flakes were recovered during the two-day excavation.

In Locality B three hearths, lying within a four-foot radius of one another, were encountered during excavation, and much of the cultural material was in direct association with the charcoal/soil matrix of the hearths. The hearth fill was recovered as three individual, bulk samples and the charcoal separated from the soil in the laboratory. None of the hearths yielded the minimum amount of charcoal required for a reliable standard (as opposed to AMS) radiometric date, so the charcoal from all three hearths was combined to produce a sample of sufficient size. We felt secure in doing this because all of the hearths had contained the basal sections of projectile points and all of the points were of the same style, suggesting contemporaneity of the hearths. The combined charcoal was submitted for radiocarbon dating by the standard method and yielded a date of 7620 ± 95 years BP (DIC-1589)[5]. This date led us to believe that the site was not of Pleistocene age, and therefore not Paleoindian, even though the small

---

[5] Charcoal collected from another hearth in 1989 returned a date of 9730 ± 80 BP (Beta-36805). This made us suspect that there might be a problem with the 7620 ± 95 BP (DIC-1589) date. In 1992 we had an archived portion of the original 1979 sample dated by the AMS method and it returned a date of 10,060 BP (Beta-52606). Based on these and subsequent dates we believe the original date of 7620 ± 95 BP to be incorrect due to laboratory error.

lithic assemblage recovered through excavation and surface collection appeared to be technologically and morphologically classic High Plains Paleoindian.

In 1980 we conducted systematic testing at the Mesa to determine the location and extent of the cultural deposit, and to identify areas of concentrated human activity. A total of 503 four-foot square excavation units were laid out across the site, and a shovel/screen testing program employed. Each square was tested by removing a single scoop of soil from the center of the square with a #2 round point shovel. The soil was then passed through a one-quarter inch mesh screen to see if it contained cultural material. The results were recorded on the grid map and the cultural material collected. The 503 gridded squares covered 23% of the area that we considered level enough to reasonably assume it might have been utilized by the ancient occupants of the site. One hundred thirty-three (26%) of the 503 tested squares yielded cultural material: three projectile points, a few biface fragments, and several hundred waste flakes. During the testing process we were also able to collect data regarding the natural stratigraphy, including looking for evidence of post-depositional disturbances in the soil profiles. In addition, a single square was excavated in Locality B.

Between 1981 and 1988, little more than annual monitoring activities were conducted at the site. In 1989 we returned to the Mesa for two days of limited excavation to collect more data regarding the geology and stratigraphy of the site. Excavation was initiated in three squares, two in Locality B and one in Locality Saddle, however the excavation of these squares was not completed until 1991. Excavation of the Saddle square revealed a small amount of charcoal (subsequent excavation in 1991 revealed this to be a hearth), which was recovered in association with cultural material. In the years that had elapsed since 1980, when the original and only radiometric determination at the site had been made, accelerator mass spectrometry (AMS) radiocarbon dating, a more refined dating method that could date very small samples, had become commercially available. We submitted the charcoal for a radiocarbon age determination utilizing the new AMS method. The charcoal from the Saddle square produced a date of 9730 ± 80 years BP (Beta-36805), approximately 2000 years older than the original date for the site. The new date indicated that the site was Pleistocene in age, and fell within the temporal range of Paleoindian sites in mid-continent North America. This was the first solid evidence to support the possibility that the Mesa might represent a Paleoindian occupation.

In an effort to corroborate the 9730 BP radiocarbon date, we returned to the site in 1991 with a small crew. In ten days we completed the excavation of the three squares started in 1989 and excavated ten additional squares, three in Locality A, two in Locality Saddle, and five in Locality B. The excavations revealed two hearths: one, in Locality A, with a fragmentary, pot-lid fractured projectile point and waste flakes incorporated in the charcoal matrix; the other in Locality Saddle, with an associated projectile point, biface fragments, and several thousand waste flakes. The charcoal/soil matrix of each hearth was collected and the charcoal extracted by hand under a microscope in the laboratory. Charcoal from these two hearths produced AMS radiocarbon dates of 10,090 ± 85 years BP (Beta-50428) and 9945 ± 75 years BP (Beta-50430). These results added more support to the probability that the site was associated with the Paleoindian tradition.

In 1992 we excavated 16 squares, eight in Locality A, seven in Locality B, and one in Locality Saddle. This work produced projectile points, biface fragments, flake tools, and waste flakes associated with ten hearths. Nine of the hearths were located in Locality B and five of them were dated. A single hearth was located in Locality Saddle and was dated. All the hearths were dated by the AMS method, and five returned dates ranging from 10,240 to 9930 years BP. Charcoal from the sixth hearth produced a date of 11,660 ± 80 years BP (Beta-55286), about 1500 years older than the average date for the site. A second sample from this hearth returned a date of 11,190 ± 70 years BP

(Beta-57430). For the first time, obsidian flakes were recovered, presenting the possibility of corroborating the age of the site by dating it independently, using the obsidian hydration method.

In 1993, 11.75 squares were excavated during the three-week field season, revealing five hearths with associated projectile points, flake tools, and waste flakes. Bulk charcoal/soil samples were recovered from each hearth and the charcoal later separated out in the laboratory. Four hearths were located in Locality B, two of which were dated. A single hearth located in Locality Saddle was also dated. Charcoal from the three hearths provided AMS radiocarbon dates clustering near 10,000 years BP. By this time we had recovered a fairly extensive lithic assemblage from the site. Based upon the technological aspects of the assemblage and the site's radiocarbon chronology, there was little doubt that the Mesa Complex was a cultural component of the Paleoindian tradition. We had also determined, as a result of the kinds of artifacts recovered and the site's location, that the primary function of the Mesa had been as a hunting lookout. Since no camping, cooking, or refuse build-up from daily living activities had occurred, the site could not provide a lot of information regarding the climate, environment, and ecology of the region during the late Pleistocene. As a result, information of this type had to be derived from data collected at off-site locales. Beginning with the 1993 field season, an intensive effort to collect this type of information was begun and continued annually for the next six years.

The 1994 field season was three weeks in length, during which time we excavated a total of 20 squares, ten in Locality A, eight in Locality B, and two in the newly designated East Ridge Locality. Through this work we recovered numerous formal and incidental artifacts, as well as thousands of waste flakes. Although we encountered no hearths during this field season, we did note several small clusters of heat-fractured artifacts. This context suggested that the artifacts had been associated with a hearth, but that subsequently the charcoal and burned soil had weathered away, leaving behind only the burned artifacts. Excavation in Locality A also revealed the presence of microblades, artifacts which had heretofore not been recognized as a component of the site assemblage. Organic material that was collected from several geologic sections near the Mesa was submitted for radiocarbon dating, as we initiated work on the development of a regional chronologic framework for the climate and ecological shifts that occurred during the Pleistocene/Holocene transition.

Beginning in 1995 we increased the length of our field seasons at the Mesa. The 1995 field season was four weeks long, and a total of 26.5 squares were excavated during that time; 13.5 in Locality A, 11 in Locality B and two in the East Ridge Locality. This work produced numerous artifacts and waste flakes and also revealed two hearths, one in Locality A, the other in Locality B. Projectile points, bifaces, incidental tools, and waste flakes were recovered from the charcoal/soil matrix of the hearths. Charcoal extracted from the hearth fill returned dates of ca. 10,000 years BP. Work continued on the paleoecological aspect of the project, primarily at a locale referred to as "Lake of the Pleistocene" (LOP) on the Etivluk River 15 miles west of the Mesa. LOP is an ancient lake that was drained about 5000 years ago. Since that time the lake sediments have remained frozen. Preliminary work at the site indicated the lake bottom sediments could provide an uninterrupted paleoecological record for the region as far back as 45,000 years BP.

In 1996 we excavated a total of 32.5 squares during a five-week field season. All but two of these squares were excavated in Locality A. One square each was excavated in Locality Saddle and Locality B. As a result of this work, a large number of formal and incidental artifacts, as well as thousands of waste flakes were recovered. Much of the cultural material was in association with the four hearths that were revealed through excavation. Three of the hearths were in Locality A and one in Locality Saddle. The Locality Saddle hearth was not dated but the three from Locality A were,

yielding dates of 10,230 ± 60 years BP (Beta-95600), 10,130 ± 60 years BP (Beta-95914), and 10,080 ± 60 years BP (Beta-95913). Paleoecological work continued at Lake of the Pleistocene and several other geologic sections in the region. A good radiocarbon-based chronologic framework was being developed for LOP, especially the period we were interested in, ca. 13,500 to 8000 years BP. Sediment samples were being collected for pollen studies, loss-on-ignition analysis, and various physical analyses.

We spent almost ten weeks in the field in 1997, during which time we excavated 28.5 squares, all of which were in Locality A. Although no hearths were encountered, we recovered numerous formal and incidental artifacts, as well as thousands of waste flakes. Paleoecological work continued at LOP and other locales. Data from this work was starting to produce a picture of what the regional ecosystem was like at the time the Mesa Paleoindians were present.

In 1998 we spent nine weeks working at the Mesa. During that period we excavated a total of 24.5 squares: five in Locality A, two in Locality B, six and a half in Locality Saddle, and 11 in the East Ridge Locality. As a result of this work, 11 hearths were revealed. Seven of the hearths were in Locality Saddle. Three were dated, averaging about 9900 years BP. Four hearths were excavated in the East Ridge Locality and three of them were dated, returning an average age of 9900 years BP. Numerous formal and incidental artifacts, and thousands of waste flakes were recovered. Much of the cultural material was directly associated with the hearths. We continued to gather paleoecological data from Lake of the Pleistocene and other geologic sections, and expanded our work to include the collection of Pleistocene megafauna fossils to provide information regarding subsistence resources available to the Mesa's inhabitants.

In 1999 we spent three weeks at the Mesa excavating a total of 15.25 squares. During this work we encountered two hearths; both were in Locality Saddle and both were dated, returning assays of 9950 ± 60 years BP (Beta-133354) and 10,180 ± 60 years BP (Beta-133353). Numerous formal and informal artifacts and thousands of waste flakes were recovered, some of which were directly associated with the hearths. We also continued our paleoecological and Pleistocene megafauna data gathering activities. This field season marked the end of field work at the Mesa. A total of 202.5 squares (3240 square feet), have been excavated revealing 40 hearths, 864 formal and incidental artifacts and 120,602 waste flakes.

MESA COMPLEX LITHIC TYPOLOGY/TECHNOLOGY

Bifaces and the byproducts of their manufacture make up the majority of the lithic assemblage at the Mesa. As such, they are the primary source of information regarding tool organization. Variability in the form of the bifaces — whether they are finished tools and where they fit in a technological sequence — is crucial in identifying different patterns of tool use. In order to compare the artifacts and pattern of organization at the site, a typology was developed which tracks variability in biface production and transport. This section will describe the typology which has been developed from the Mesa assemblage.

Bifacial Tools

Bifaces are defined as pieces which are wider than they are thick and have two readily recognizable flaked surfaces. Those pieces which fit the definition of bifaces total 366, and can be divided into two main categories: finished formal types and manufacture failures. The classification scheme for discriminating between these categories, and for identifying different classes within the category of finished bifaces, is based on five presence/absence attributes: 1) comedial flaking, 2) base shaping, 3) tip shaping, 4) edge grinding, and 5) edge retouch. Comedial flaking describes the final flaking pattern, where flakes are generally parallel and terminate at the centerline, producing a ridge down the length of the piece. Base and tip shaping describe the formation of bifaces into projectile points with a distinct base/tip orientation. Other bifaces may be pointed, but they do not have a flak-

ing pattern designed to produce a tip. The pointed end results from the convergence of two straight sides. Edge grinding and edge retouch describe different methods of tool finishing. Edge grinding is a characteristic of projectile points, where the lower portion of the lateral edges are ground smooth, presumably to aid in hafting. Edge retouch describes the removal of small pressure flakes around the perimeter of a piece which serve to straighten and even the edge and provide final shaping (Bever 2000).

Finished bifaces

Different combinations of these attributes identify three distinct types. These are: projectile points, type A bifaces and type B bifaces. Each represents a unique combination of presence/absence attributes, and a distinct shape. Although these formal types are defined on the basis of attributes which do not reflect shape and size, they are quite distinctive in form. In general, projectile points are smaller and narrower than type A and B bifaces. Type A bifaces are relatively thick, and they cluster more tightly than projectile points along the ratio of width:thickness. This is simply a reflection of the robust comedial flaking in type A bifaces which produces a pronounced diamond-shaped cross-section. In contrast, type B bifaces are the thinnest relative to width, although they tend to be larger and sometimes thinner than projectile points. While there is certainly overlap, when combined with the attributes of flaking, shaping and edge retouch, it becomes clear that these are distinct types (Bever 2000).

projectile points

The bifacial inventory of the Mesa is dominated by projectile points of which there are 154 complete and fragmentary examples. Typical points are recognized by the presence of comedial flaking, the formation of a distinct base and tip, and edge grinding. Of course, all four of these attributes are not always present on all of the pieces. In fact, most of the points are broken fragments, predominantly bases. A point base, for example, lacks data on tip shaping. Most of the pieces are large enough that they retain evidence of either base or tip formation, or edge grinding, and the combination of only a few of the attributes identifies pieces as points.

In general, projectile points are lanceolate in outline, with parallel flakes perpendicular to the long axis of the point, which results in a ridge down the centerline of the point (Figure 19 & 20), creating a lenticular to diamond-shaped cross-section. Most bases show evidence of thinning leading to a concave shape, though bases range from deeply concave with distinct ears, to convex, rounded forms. A few of the points exhibit the removal of longitudinal flakes from the base, which could be construed as fluting or an attempt to flute. However, most "fluting" appears to be more incidental than purposeful. In the points with concave and straight bases, numerous minute hinge-fractures are present along the basal margin. These fractures may result from movement of the point within the haft. This could indicate that a different style of hafting was used for convex based points, which do not display as much basal hinge fracturing. While there may be meaningful variability in base form, for this report all points will be treated as one type. All of the points are similar in outline, cross-section, and flaking pattern, and heavy edge grinding is present on all but a few. More than 75 percent of the points with the relevant portion present, show evidence of extensive reworking, which creates a distinct shoulder. Most of the points show

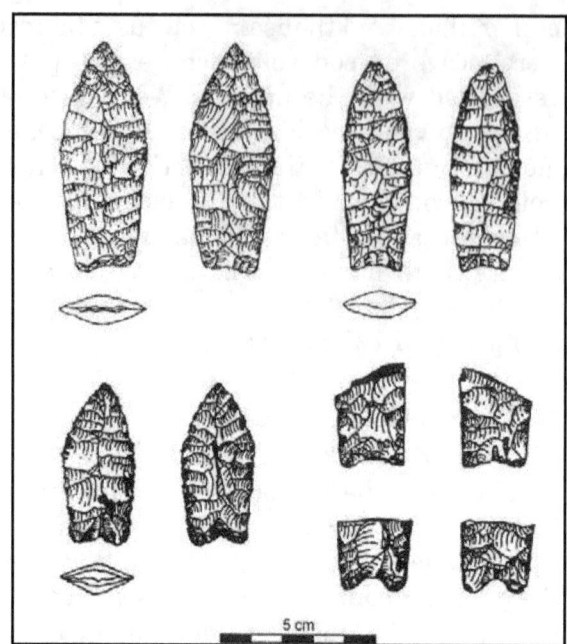

Figure 20. Mesa projectile points showing both faces, cross section, and variation in basal treatment. (After Bever 2000)

signs of impact damage, and presumably were broken in use as projectile points (Bever 2000).

In addition to the typical points, there are seven points that do not have edge grinding. Although a lack of edge grinding may indicate that the pieces broke before they were finished, there are a few points in the assemblage which lack edge grinding but have impact fractures and evidence of use. An additional four pieces have edge grinding and the general outline of a Mesa projectile point, but they lack comedial flaking. Because they do not differ in overall shape, and presumably serve the same function as points, they are also included in the projectile point category.

Finally, 21 point tips are recognized that lack evidence of comedial flaking. While definitely projectile points, it is not clear if they are finished specimens or pieces broken in a late stage of manufacture. If finished, the pieces may have broken too close to the end of the point to recognize flaking pattern, or they are reworked tips, which tend to have more uneven flaking. On the other hand, they may be late stage manufacture breaks. Given the large amount of point production that occurred on-site, it would be surprising if there were not a few

Figure 19. Complete and reworked Mesa projectile points. (Photo: R. Reanier)

points that broke during the final stages of manufacture.

Based upon metric data from complete and reconstructed specimens, finished projectile points appear to have ranged in length from 50 to 100mm, in width from 16 to 28mm, and in thickness from 5 to 10mm (25mm = 1 inch). Although we have no hard evidence, the size and robust character of the projectile points suggest they were used to tip atlatl darts. Most of the points appear to be too large or heavy to be used as arrowheads, and at the same time are smaller than points usually attributed to lances or spears. Mesa projectile points are purposefully robust and are probably designed that way to facilitate reworking. More than twenty specimens recovered from the site have been resharpened in the haft at least once, an activity that seems to have been a common field expedient. Given the uneven, often frozen surface of the landscape, missed casts may often have resulted in broken and damaged points. The robust points apparently had a reasonably good survival rate. Some of the reworked points may also have been used as hafted knives (Bever 2000).

The style and shape of the Mesa projectile points are similar to the points of the Agate Basin Complex of the High Plains (Kunz and Reanier 1995). The practice of reworking broken and damaged points is as common in Agate Basin and other Paleoindian Complexes, as it is in Mesa. The technological relationship between the two complexes is easily recognized because they are both Paleoindian. The possibility of a stronger relationship has been discussed elsewhere (see Kunz and Reanier 1995) and will not be addressed here.

type A bifaces

What we have classified as the non-projectile point bifaces recovered from the site have been divided into two types, A and B. There are 14 type A bifaces. Like the projectile points, they have comedial flaking, but are not edge ground; they lack evidence of base and tip shaping, and most have edge retouch. Though most are broken, all of the pieces are long, narrow and pointed, with straight sides. Like the projectile points, the

flaking pattern consists of robust parallel-opposed flakes terminating at the centerline, creating a strong diamond-shaped cross-section and a distinct ridge running the full length of the piece. Their large size and tapering sides, however, rule out the possibility that they are projectile point preforms, of which there are many examples in the Mesa assemblage. One complete example and one partially reconstructed from several fragments suggest that the pieces were pointed on both ends. Based upon metric data from the one complete and one reconstructed specimen, these artifacts range in length from 85 to 130mm, in width from 19 to 36mm, and in thickness 8 to 15mm. At present the function of these tools is unknown, although use-wear, residue, and other types of analyses are expected to provide additional information.

type B bifaces

There are 20 type B bifaces, all have edge retouch and lack comedial flaking (Figure 21). In general, these bifaces are larger, wider, somewhat thinner, and manufactured in a different manner, than the other finished bifaces. They are quite well made, and reduction was accomplished through the removal of large percussion flakes, often extending across most or all of the face. Their method of manufacture differs from

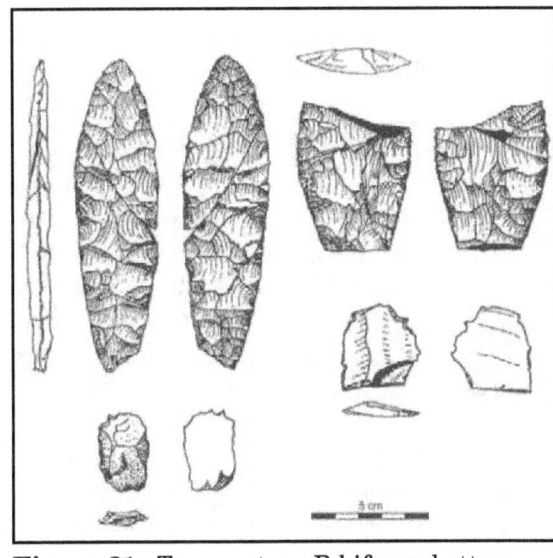

Figure 21. Top row type B bifaces; bottom row; gravers. (After Bever 2000)

projectile points and type A bifaces, which were generally finished with robust pressure flakes terminating at the centerline.

The intent for type B bifaces seems to have been to thin the pieces, rather than create a thick, robust biface as exemplified by the points. Though most are broken, in outline these bifaces tend to be wide and pointed with fairly straight sides. They are interpreted as finished, because they have fine pressure retouch along the edges, forming a straight, even edge. It is also worth noting that some are manufactured on non-local material. Two complete examples show that these tools may have been bipointed and leaf- or lance-shaped in outline. Based upon metric data from complete and fragmentary specimens, finished examples appear to have ranged in length from 130 to 165mm, in width from 38 to 50mm, and in thickness from 4 to 8mm.

Our analysis concerning these tools is incomplete and their function remains unknown. Their size and shape suggest they may have been used as knives, but use as lance points is also a possiblity (Bever 2000). It is also interesting that almost all of the primary and secondary flaking (with the exception of fine edge retouch) was achieved by percussion flaking. This is especially notable because of the large size and thinness of the tools. This technique is much like that employed by Clovis tool makers (Bradley 1993; Boldurian and Cotter 1999; Collins 1999). Some of these bifaces are simular to those recovered from the Tuluaq Hill Site (Rasic 2000).

Unfinished bifaces

The preceding discussion pertains to a category of bifaces which are considered to be finished, or formal bifaces. A second category of bifaces includes those which were broken or rejected during manufacture. While ultimately they might have become formal bifaces, they did not progress to that point, and as such, they comprise a second category of bifacial artifacts. These biface failures occur in frequencies second only to projectile points. Since they lack the attributes of finished tools, they are not formal tools and are considered separately from the pre-

viously described forms. These biface failures are quite variable in shape, size and flaking pattern, due in part to breakage, but also to variation in technology and the degree of reduction. Because they form a large portion of the bifacial inventory, and because they reflect a large segment of on-site activities, they have been subdivided based on reduction stage (Bever 2000). Early and late stage examples form the largest percentage of the manufacture failures, and describe a rather arbitrary division along the continuum between recognizable stages of reduction.

early stage failures

There are 30 bifaces in the early stage failure class. These artifacts have few and large flake scars, but show that a purposeful reduction process had been initiated. Assuming that they were discarded before completion, with further reduction they could have become either of the late stage pieces, and hence, potentially different finished types.

late stage failures/projectile point preforms

There are 83 examples of late stage failures. These artifacts can be described as projectile point preforms, but also include examples that are finely flaked and symmetrical. Because of their high width:thickness ratio, and the fact that they are in a later stage of reduction but are not comedially flaked, they are most similar to unfinished type B bifaces.

crude biface failures

Crude biface failures number 20 and are large and thick and have only a few large flakes removed from either surface. They were broken or discarded at a stage of manufacture where it is impossible to determine what the final product might have been (Bever 2000).

uncategorized bifaces

There are 45 uncategorized bifaces which are pieces too burned or weathered to provide sorting attributes, and edge fragments which are pieces, probably biface failures, that are too fragmentary to provide categorizing information.

Unifacial Tools

Unifacial tools display flake removal scars on only one surface and fall into two general categories: a single type of formal scraper, and informal flake tools. Generally speaking, flake tools are informal. This means there is no patterning in blank form and the retouch is not standardized, but simply creates a working edge or bit. Blanks for flake tools are typically waste flakes which show no specific preparation for a particular type of tool, although certain types of flakes were more likely to be chosen for certain types of tools by the user. Flake tools were categorized based on the type of flake which forms the blank, as well as the form of the retouch (Bever 2000).

Formal tools
scrapers

The category of formal unifacial tools is comprised solely of scrapers. These differ from other flake tools in that most are quite large and were produced on thick flakes with flat ventral surfaces (Figure 22). The blanks they were made from are not waste flakes, but seem to have been purposefully produced for use as scrapers. In contrast to the rather expedient flake tools, formal scrapers tend to be well made, with a flak-

Figure 22. Examples of scrapers recovered from the Mesa. (Photo: M. Kunz)

ing pattern as coordinated as that seen on finished bifaces. Indeed, some of the pieces were bifacially worked prior to the formation of a steep scraping edge. Though some are broken fragments, most appear to have been symmetrical and ovate in shape, with a steep scraping edge around the entire perimeter of the piece. Given their large size and the fact that some are broken into fragments, they may also have been used for tasks other than scraping. Formal scrapers and suitably sized flake blanks occur primarily in Locality East Ridge. A total of six scrapers were recovered from the site.

Informal tools
gravers

Gravers are flakes with delicate, retouched spurs (Figure 21). These tools usually have one spur, but examples with multiple spurs are not uncommon. Most of the gravers are also retouched along a portion of the flake edge. Gravers were probably used for incising, scribing, drilling/boring, perforating, and as mini marlinspikes, and are generally thought to be associated with preparation and repair of hunting equipment (Boast 1983). There are a total of 70 gravers in the Mesa assemblage. Although in this report gravers are classified as informal tools, perhaps semi-formal would be a more accurate designation. While no preordained blank was made to produce gravers it is obvious that the flakes utilized to make this tool generally possess certain attributes. Although flakes with the required attributes could be found among the debitage, the selection process went well beyond that of simply grabbing any handy waste flake as would be the case with retouched or utilized flakes. The purposes for which they were used required gravers to be delicate but at the same time withstand extreme pressure. As a result, in use they often snapped and most of the gravers recovered from the Mesa are broken. The few that are not broken or have been reconstructed from fragments, suggest that they were usually made on flakes which provided a natural tang or handle to facilitate their use. In fact some gravers may have been hafted, a circumstance that would definitely remove them from the informal tool category.

flake scrapers

Also present are larger, thicker flakes which display relatively robust retouch flake removal, producing a steeply angled edge, similar to scraper retouch. We call these flake scrapers. Although flake scrapers are not a formal type because they are quite variable in shape, the larger retouch scars are distinctive and separate them from simple retouched flakes. Thirteen of these tools were recovered from the Mesa.

flake burins

Flakes which have burinated edges are referred to as flake burins. Unlike many other Alaskan sites that contain formal or stylized burins, the burinated flakes at the Mesa are very few in number, and show no distinctive patterning in either the method of burination or in blank form. Although the burination seems intentional, they are probably tools of opportunity and are not considered a formal type. Six of these artifacts occur in the Mesa assemblage (Bever 2000).

retouched/utilized flakes

The retouched or utilized flake category includes all of those pieces that have continuous retouch (five or more retouch scars) along a portion or portions of the flake edge. The differences between those pieces that show signs of definite retouch versus flaking caused by use are often not obvious, and both of these tools have been grouped into one type. A total of 237 retouched/utilized flakes are found in the Mesa assemblage.

Flaking Detritus

Excavation at the Mesa produced 120,602 pieces of flaking detritus. Because the amount is so large only a representative sample of 17,272 flakes (14%) has been analyzed. Although a variety of metric and categorical attributes were recorded for flaking debris, each flake was also assigned to a discrete type, in a manner similar to that for the formal bifaces.

Though the largest flakes are clearly the product of percussion flaking, and the smallest bifacial flakes the result of pressure flaking, there is much variability in between. These different techniques of flake reduction were not explored in detail for this report, nor was data on flaking mode, such as soft versus hard hammer.

Flake fragments

Flakes large enough to have a recognizable dorsal/ventral surface were categorized based on the presence or absence of a striking platform or platform remnant. Since most attributes which identify flake technology stem from platform morphology, those flakes which lack platforms are assigned to a group called flake fragments. These are typically medial or distal fragments that could not be assigned to a particular technological category. There are 12,594 examples of this flake type in the sample accounting for 72.9% of the total.

Flakes with platforms

Flakes with platforms (i.e. complete and proximal specimens) were assigned to different classes based on several attributes found to be useful in a number of experimental studies (see Amick and Mauldin 1989). Platforms were divided into the following types: 1) bifacial, 2) non-bifacial, and 3) cortical.

Not surprisingly, a substantially higher frequency of bifacial flakes exhibit some form of preparation; this is typical in bifacial technologies that produce well-made, standardized tools like Mesa projectile points. With the exception of primary flakes, most flakes in the assemblage are very small, whether broken or complete. While many flakes are broken, a fairly large percentage of the flakes comprise complete or proximal fragments. For all flake types, slightly more than 87% are smaller than 1.5 cm in maximum dimension. Among these flakes, 31.6% retain platforms. For flakes larger than 1.5 cm, complete or proximal fragments form a substantial portion. This suggests that the small size of the flakes — regardless of whether they retain a platform

— reflects patterns of reduction rather than post-depositional breakage (Bever 2000).

Bifacial flakes

The vast majority of the flakes in the assemblage are the product of bifacial reduction. Bifacial flakes are characterized by acute, faceted platforms formed from the edge of a biface and numbered 4,063 or 23.5% of the sample. Flake scars tend to be multidirectional, with diffuse, feathered scar edges and indistinct arrises. The flakes are relatively thin and gently curved in cross-section.

Non-bifacial flakes

In contrast, single facet and particularly multifacet flakes are few in number, and neither class exhibits patterning in morphology indicative of different types of core reduction. In this analysis, both have been combined into a single type, termed non-bifacial flakes which total 416 or 2.4% of the sample. Though these flakes lack bifacial platforms, they are not necessarily indicative of a non-bifacial technology. As a group they are rather amorphous, but many may actually be the product of bifacial reduction.

Cortical flakes

Flakes with cortical platforms are generally larger, and very often, most of the dorsal surface retains cortex. These are referred to as primary flakes. Because they derive from the earliest stages of nodule shaping, these flakes could be considered either bifacial or non-bifacial. Thirty-one examples of this flake type make up 0.2% of the sample (Bever 2000).

Shatter

Small angular fragments, so small that the dorsal/ventral surfaces cannot be determined are termed shatter, and were assigned to a separate group. There are 168 examples in this category which is 1% of the sample.

Flake Cores

Relative to the number of flakes, flake cores are extremely rare in the assemblage,

with only two pieces which clearly functioned as flake cores. Both are informal, with no evidence of a particular orientation, method of preparation, or regularity in products. Because flake cores are so few in number, they are clearly not a regular part of the technology of the Mesa Complex as viewed at the Mesa site. Sixty-five other items which might presumably have been intended to be cores are simply chunks or tabular nodules with only a few flake removals. Most of these occur on poor quality raw material nodules which were either quickly discarded, or shattered upon flaking, producing neither a functional core nor useable blanks. In most cases, it seems these pieces were intended to be bifaces. They simply shattered before reaching an advanced stage of reduction.

Other Cultural Material

In addition to the flaked-stone material discussed in the preceding section there are several other categories of cultural material that bear mentioning. Fifty-nine manuports — items that do not naturally occur on the Mesa and could have gotten there only by human transport — were recovered from the site. Almost all of these (N=51) are unaltered stream cobbles some of which display signs that they were used as hammer stones, although several appear to be heat fractured. There are also several large, flat pieces of stone. Some appear to have been used as anvils, while others are simply exotic material. Eleven quartz crystals and flakes of quartz are present in the assemblage. While the gabbro bedrock of the Mesa contains some quartz inclusions, we have not seen any that are greater than 10mm in diameter. It is our assumption that these 11 examples were brought to the Mesa by people utilizing the site. Five pieces of orange hematite were also recovered. There is some indication of abrasion on several of the pieces, which may indicate they had been used in some manner for coloring. All of this material appears to be associated with the Paleoindian occupation of the Mesa.

In the following section another lithic assemblage, a microblade component, will be discussed. This component is not part of the Mesa Complex, but is part of the site assemblage. Also not part of the Mesa Complex is a .44-40 W.C.F. brass cartridge case, which was recovered on the surface in Locality A. This artifact suggests use of the site, probably as a vantage point, around 1880 by Nunamiut Eskimos (Adkins 1994). Other similar artifacts and features in the region are associated with Nunamiut activity prior to 1950. In addition, 142 gastroliths — stones from bird crops — were found at the site. This may indicate that the human inhabitants of the Mesa had a taste for ptarmigan but we suspect most of the stones are due to the activity of non-human predators or the result of other types of natural bird mortality.

THE MESA SITE MICROBLADE COMPONENT

The Mesa assemblage contains a relatively narrow range of artifact types, which are found across the site, and co-occur within each locality. These consist primarily of projectile points, bifaces, waste flakes, and informal flake tools, and have been assigned to the Mesa Paleoindian Complex as described in the previous section. The artifacts are assumed to represent one cultural component and their function exemplifies site use.

However, there is evidence of another cultural component at the site, which is unrelated to the Paleoindian occupation, and is more recent in age. This component is identified most readily by microblades, microblade core fragments, and a wedge-

Figure 23. Artifacts from Mesa microblade component: (a) fluted biface, (b) core fragments, (c) wedge-shaped microblade core, and (d) microblades. (Photo: M. Kunz)

shaped microblade core (Figure 23). It also contains at least four bifaces, a number of possible microblade core preparation elements, and several hundred non-diagnostic waste flakes. One of these bifaces is unequivocally fluted. Described and illustrated in Kunz and Reanier (1995), this piece has been fluted on both faces, and from both ends. Though fluting is generally viewed as a Paleoindian trait, this fluted piece is not typical of the bifacial artifacts in the Mesa Complex. For reasons discussed below, it is probably associated with the microblade occupation of the Mesa, and as such, is not related to the Mesa Paleoindian Complex (Bever 2000).

Another unique artifact was found associated with the site's microblade component in Sublocality A3. This lithic artifact is round and relatively flat with a hole passing through its center. It is ca. 12.5mm thick and 38mm in diameter. We refer to it as the "roller skate wheel" (Figure 24). The artifact shows little evidence of human alter-

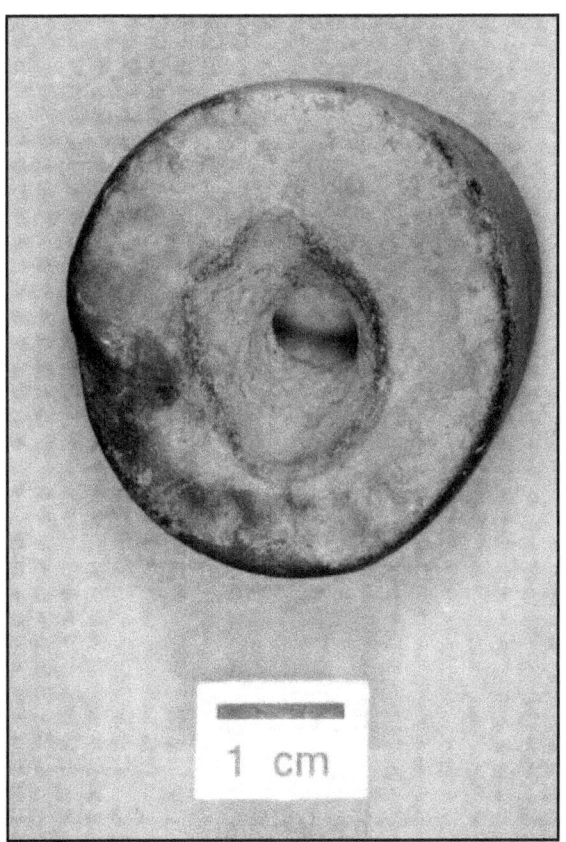

Figure 24. Circular stone artifact referred to as the "roller skate wheel". (Photo: R.E. Reanier)

ation, and may have been brought to the site as a natural curiosity. Although we have no direct evidence for its use, we speculate that it could have served as a pendant or perhaps as an atlatl weight.

The delineation of the microblade component from the rest of the Mesa assemblage was necessary in order to ensure that the artifacts from this occupation would not be confused with those of the Paleoindian component. While the microblade component certainly provides information relevant to the prehistory of the North Slope, it is not the purpose of this report to explore the details of the microblade occupation, but simply to identify the artifacts associated with that occupation and distinguish them from the Mesa Paleoindian component.

Microblades and other artifacts associated with the microblade occupation are only present in Locality A, and occur primarily in the southern portion of Sublocality A1/2. All but eight of the 130 microblade fragments come from this area, as well as most of the waste flakes associated with the microblade component. The fluted biface was also found within the cluster of microblades in Sublocality A1/2. A smaller number of artifacts that relate to the microblade component, also occur in the northwestern portion of Sublocality A4, and fewer still in Sublocalities A-5 and A-3. While the diagnostic artifacts of the microblade component (microblades, microblade core fragments, and microblade core preparation flakes) are readily recognizable, the non-diagnostic pieces associated with the occupation (waste flakes and bifaces) are more difficult to identify. Both the spatial distribution, and raw material characteristics of the artifacts were used to distinguish them from the Paleoindian Mesa Assemblage (Bever 2000).

Figure 25 shows the distribution of artifacts in the sublocalities of Locality A. The microblades occupy a relatively small area. Based simply on this distribution, there is clear separation between the area containing the microblades, and the main concentration of debris related to the Paleoindian occupation. Aside from artifacts indicative of the microblade occupation, tools related

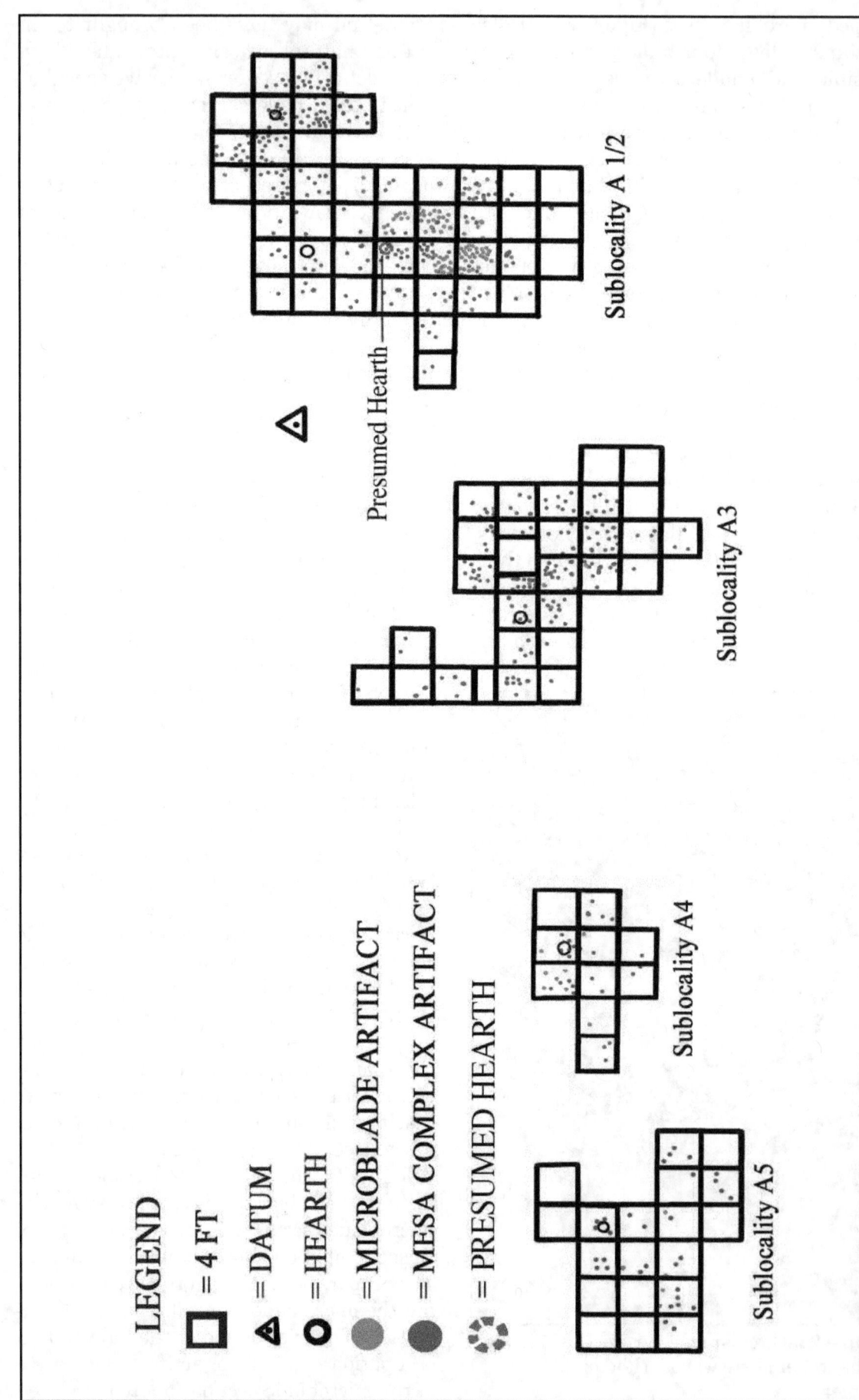

Figure 25. Distribution of microblade component artifacts in relation to location of Mesa Complex artifacts and hearths.

to the Paleoindian occupation (e.g. points and gravers) also occur within the microblade scatter, indicating that there is spatial overlap between the two components. Additionally, there were several burned flakes and a burned biface found clustered together in square (S9-13/E16-20), suggesting that a hearth may have existed there at one time. No microblades occur in this presumed hearth. The center of the microblade concentration lies about seven feet to the south of the presumed hearth artifact cluster. Without question, the tool and debitage concentration in this hearth relates to the Paleoindian occupation as it mirrors the pattern of Paleoindian debitage in hearth-fill seen repeatedly across the rest of the site.

To investigate this overlap between the microblade and Paleoindian components in more detail, we examined the raw material characteristics of both the microblades and waste flakes in this area. In the site assemblage, microblades occur on seven different raw materials. About a third of the microblades are made from two local materials, black and tan chert. These materials, particularly the black chert, are common in both the Paleoindian and microblade components of the site assemblage. The local black chert is the primary lithic material used at the site, and accounts for the majority of the Paleoindian artifacts found scattered across the site. Core preparation flakes are also made from this chert. Excluding these two local materials, the majority of the microblades are made from raw materials that do not show up elsewhere in the site assemblage on diagnostic Paleoindian artifacts. Two of these exotic materials are represented by only three microblades. Since these materials do not occur anywhere else in the site assemblage, they provide little utility in defining the distribution of the microblade occupation (Bever 2000).

In combination, the remaining two exotic materials, a maroon chert and a translucent gray chert, account for more than half of the microblades in the assemblage. Both of these materials are also found on flaking debris in all the sublocalities of Locality A.

Both these cherts are rare in the site assemblage, which suggest they are not locally available (Gil Mull, personal communication 1997). The source of the gray chert is unknown, but the maroon chert likely derives from the DeLong Mountains. The nearest known quality outcrop is 60 miles west along the Kuna River. Importantly, neither of these materials shows up in the assemblage as diagnostic Mesa Complex artifacts, and nowhere are they clearly associated with a dated Mesa Complex hearth. These cherts do not seem to have been used by the Paleoindian occupants of the Mesa, and probably provide a clear indication of the distribution of the microblade component.

The translucent gray chert only occurs in Sublocality A1/2, found as microblades and spatially associated waste flakes. As such, the microblades and flakes of this material clearly relate to the same episode of site use. The translucent gray flakes are either very small chips or small bifacial pressure flakes. This suggests that in addition to microblade production, there was also some bifacial reduction occuring during the microblade occupation.

Other artifacts are also made of the maroon chert. In addition to the microblades and flaking debris, the fluted biface is made from maroon chert. Because the material is non-local, occurs spatially associated with microblades of the same material, and does not occur on any typical diagnostic Mesa Complex artifacts, it seems reasonable to conclude that this fluted biface is a product of the microblade occupation. In fact, the maroon flakes in Sublocality A1/2 are small chips and pressure flakes, and while no direct refits could be found, it seems likely that they relate to the manufacture of the fluted biface. They are of the correct size, morphology, and color patterning. This analysis indicates that the fluted biface is not associated with the Paleoindian occupation, as originally believed (Kunz and Reanier 1995), but instead with the microblade occupation (Bever 2000).

The non-local maroon chert from the microblade component shows up elsewhere at the site as well. Nowhere, however, is it spatially associated with any Paleoindian materials or a dated hearth, and nowhere does it show up as a point, biface, graver, or in any other form indicating an affiliation with the Paleoindian occupation. In Sublocality A5, in fact, there are numerous waste flakes and two possible fragments of microblade cores made from this material. Sublocality A5 also contains one microblade (two fragments which refit) on a dark gray chert with a distinctive cortex. A biface fragment and several waste flakes also display this distinctive cortex, and presumably relate to the microblades. The size and well-controlled parallel flaking pattern of the biface are quite similar to the fluted piece in Sublocality A1/2. The distribution of the maroon flakes and these diagnostic artifacts is peripheral to the main concentration of Mesa Complex debris. Therefore this seems to be another manifestation of the microblade component. By virtue of the fact that both are dominated by the same rare, non-local maroon chert, they are probably related. Therefore the flakes, core fragments, microblades, and biface in Sublocality A5 are included in the microblade component.

Additional evidence of a microblade occupation is present in Sublocalities A4 and A3. Sublocality A4 contains a large concentration of typical Mesa Component debris, as well as a small, exhausted wedge-shaped core and six microblades on black chert. While these materials overlap spatially with the Paleoindian artifacts, the evidence suggests that the microblade-related pieces are a later, unrelated occupation, probably associated with the rest of the microblade component from the site. The evidence concerns one well-made biface half. The biface appears to be a typical Mesa Complex type B biface. Such bifaces are found across the site and are clearly related to the Paleoindian component. However, this biface has been altered to produce a striking platform on the fracture face. From this face several spalls (microblades) were driven off one of the lateral margins in a manner similar to a microblade core. There is no evidence of this type of activity anywhere else on the site, so its occurrence is not typical of the assemblage as a whole. It seems reasonable to suppose that this broken Mesa Complex biface was picked up by a later occupant with the intent of turning it into a microblade core (or possibly a multifaceted burin), unsuccessfully due to a flaw in the material. While the microblade component is undated, if this biface does indicate scavenging of Mesa Complex material by the microblade occupation, then the microblade component must postdate the Paleoindian occupation, though the exact age is, of course, unknown.

A small basal fragment of a notched projectile point made from black chert was also found in this area. This piece is clearly intrusive in the Mesa Complex assemblage, and presumably is associated with the microblade occupation (Bever 2000). Similar materials — wedge-shaped microblade cores, microblades, and notched points — have been dated at the Lisburne site, five miles north of the Mesa, at ca. 3500 years BP (Bowers 1999). It seems reasonable to assume that the microblade component at the Mesa is related culturally and temporally to the occupation at Lisburne.

Based on the patterns previously described, at least 707 artifacts and detrital pieces can be assigned to the microblade component. These include both diagnostic artifacts, and waste flakes on the distinctive materials discussed above. Undoubtedly, local materials found in the rest of the assemblage were used by the microblade occupation as well, minimally including the black and tan chert seen on the microblades. Presumably, some of the non-diagnostic waste flakes made from these materials belong to the microblade component as well. However, there is no way to identify them.

Although microblade component material was found associated with Mesa Complex artifacts and detritus in Locality A, none was found associated with any of the hearths or included within the charcoal/soil matrix of any hearth. This coupled with other factors previously discussed indicates that microblade technology is not part of the Mesa Complex lithic industry and represents only brief and sporadic use of the Mesa by a more recent group.

LITHIC SOURCES

Most of the information that we have gleaned through excavation of the Mesa is based upon the stone tools found there. Much of that data is directly linked to the types of stone selected for the manufacture of the tools, as well as its availability. In addition, the physical properties or litho-mechanical characteristics of the different types of stone also provide insights into the activities of the Mesa occupants, and warrants a brief discussion.

Chert is a hard, dense rock that is primarily silicon dioxide, and has a vitreous or glassy luster. When struck, it displays the property of conchoidal fracture. Occasionally, silicified mudstone and limestone are confused with, or identified as chert, and

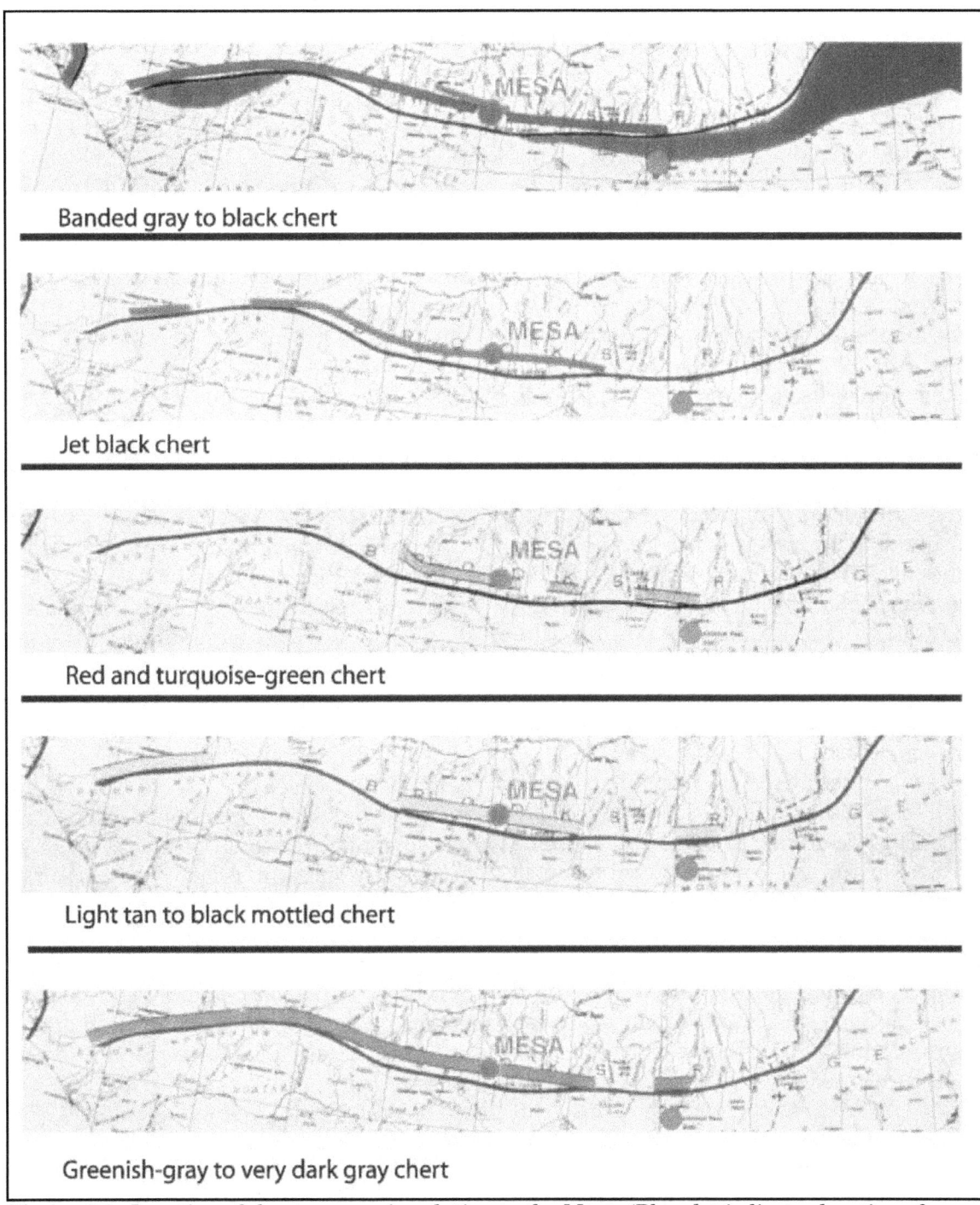

Figure 26. Location of chert sources in relation to the Mesa. (Blue dot indicates location of Anaktuvuk Pass, and heavy dark line traces the continental divide.) (After Mull 1994)

39

fine grained basalt can often display similar properties. All of these materials are present in the Brooks Range, and were used to make the stone tools found at the Mesa. However, 99% of the tools and manufacturing detritus at the site is chert. The reason is that high quality chert is abundant in the sedimentary rocks along most of the northern flank of the Brooks Range. This is particularly true in the foothills of the western and central Brooks Range, as is demonstrated by the ubiquitous occurrence of chert cobbles in every major and minor drainage flowing out of the mountains (Mull 1994). Although it has long been assumed that prehistoric peoples of the region were obtaining their tool stone primarily from the chert cobbles found in these streams, our research at the Mesa does not support that assumption. Most of the stone flakes at the site that display cortex, show a cortex of the type associated with primary deposits such as nodules, lenses, or beds. While stream cobbles were used, they do not appear to have been used as frequently as material from primary sources. The work of Shelley (1994) and John Dubé (personal communication 2001) has demonstrated that due to the harsh arctic in-stream environment, the litho-mechanical properties/quality of most stream cobbles have been substantially degraded. Therefore, at least for the Paleoindians at the Mesa, the majority of lithic procurement seems to have been carried out at primary sources, which are numerous, nearby, and readily accessible.

It is interesting to note, as pointed out by Mull (1994), that many varieties and colors of chert are confined to specific formations for which the geographic distribution is fairly well known. In some cases, such information can provide insights into the tool stone preferences and movements of prehistoric peoples of the region. However, there is probably no location along the northern flank of the Brooks Range where usable chert is not readily available. Although as Mull (1994) points out, even though the location of the Mesa is within ten miles of potential sources of most of the known Brooks Range chert types, the vast majority of the tools made by the Mesa Paleoindians are made of local chert from sources no more than a mile or two distant (Figure 26).

One tool, a graver, and 61 flakes of obsidian were recovered from the Mesa. Most of the flakes are small retouch flakes, although there are a few larger ones indicative of the bifacial reduction process. Obsidian was found in all the localities of the site, most commonly directly associated with hearths. The only obsidian source north of the Yukon River, Batza Téna, lies 200 miles to the south of the site in the Koyukuk drainage. Neutron activation and other types of trace element analysis indicate that the Mesa obsidian is from the Batza Téna source (Cook 1999; Kunz et al. 2001). The small flakes indicate that most of the obsidian (only .0005% of the total number of flakes recovered from the site) probably arrived at the Mesa in the form of finished tools. The presence of obsidian at the site suggests that the Mesa Paleoindians had a wide range of geographic knowledge of Alaska north of the Yukon River, and/or that an extensive trading network existed in the region prior to and during their occupation of the site.

SITE USE

We believe that the majority of the area of the Mesa that was used by its prehistoric occupants has been excavated. The kinds of features and artifacts found across the site (except as previously noted) are consistent. Therefore, we feel confident that the material we have gathered through excavation is, without question, representative of the primary activities that were carried out there. As previously mentioned, excavation has demonstrated that the site is comprised of a large number of relatively small activity areas, usually with a hearth or hearths as the focal point of the activity. The small activity areas cluster into larger use areas, which in general correspond to our locality and/or sublocality designations, and in turn reflect the local surface topography atop the Mesa.

The site's lithic assemblage is made up of more than 121,000 pieces, and while extensive, it lacks variety. Formal tools, which number 442 (excluding artifacts attributed to the microblade component), represent only four types: projectile points (N=154), other bifaces (N=212), gravers (N=70), and scrapers (N=6). The vast majority of the more than 120,000 waste flakes result from the process of bifacial reduction, and there is no doubt that the primary activity taking place on the Mesa was biface reduction/ projectile point manufacture.

Gravers are tools considered by most archaeologists to be the prehistoric equivalent of the Swiss Army Knife, and are most often associated with the repair and retooling of hunting equipment (Judge 1973; Boast 1983).

All but two of the scrapers are associated with the only one of 40 hearths and that hearth appears to have food preparation activities associated with it. Scrapers are usually associated with hide working, and therefore are ancillary tools in relation to the primary activity occurring at the Mesa. This would account for their low numbers.

Finally, the Mesa's morphology and location provide a wonderful vantage point from which to view a large expanse of the surrounding countryside. Taken in total, this data suggests that the Mesa was utilized as a hunting lookout.

Although we lack hard evidence, we believe the hunters who periodically occupied the Mesa likely set up a base camp along nearby Iteriak Creek, where the riparian zone provided good water, construction materials, fuel, and other comforts. Probably on a daily basis, hunters from the base camp would spend much of their time atop the Mesa scanning the surrounding landscape for game animals. Three of the four use areas (excavation localities) are situated so that an unobstructed 360° view is available. The exception occurrs at Locality Saddle, which offers a limited view northwest through northeast. This locality may have been occupied because it is somewhat sheltered from the strong winds and storms of summer, which are predominately from the south. While keeping a lookout for game, the hunters worked on their equipment, removing and discarding broken and reworked projectile points and hafting new ones.[6] This activity almost always was conducted adjacent to a small fire, which may have been

necessary to the hafting process (ie. heating mastic), for personal warmth, for a smudge against mosquitos, or all of these purposes. There is very little evidence suggesting the fires were used for cooking; we assume that activity was usually conducted at the base camp. Regardless of their purpose, the fires were an integral part of the activities at the Mesa, as indicated by the high artifact and waste flake densities surrounding them.

TOOL USE-WEAR AND RESIDUE ANALYSIS

Most functional studies of Paleoindian artifacts have concentrated on projectile points and their role as tools used in hunting and butchering animals (Kay 1996; Loy and Dixon 1998). Microscopic use-wear analysis can provide data concerning tool use not readily discernable by other means of examination, and residue analysis can often reveal evidence for exploitation of materials that does not otherwise survive in the archaeological record (Hardy and Garufi 1998; Hardy and Kay 1998). Preliminary analysis of a representative sample of the Mesa Complex lithic assemblage has been microscopically examined to obtain data that could provide additional information regarding the activities that took place on the Mesa.

The artifacts were examined using reflected light microscopy at magnifications ranging from 50 to 500 diameters using Olympus BX-60 and Olympus BX-30 microscopes (Hardy 2000, 2001). All residues and wear patterns were photographed and compared with experimental and published material for identification (Anderson-Gerfaud 1990; Hardy 1994; Hardy and Garufi 1998). Potentially recognizable residues include animal (hair, feather, skin, bone, antler, and blood) and plant (starch grains, cellular tissue, wood fragments, and phytoliths) material (Hardy 1994; Hardy and Garufi 1998; Hardy and Kay 1998). Use-wear identification is concentrated on stria-

---

6 More than 85% of the projectile points recovered from the Mesa are the snapped basal portions of points, or points that were resharpened while in the haft, presumably a field expedient.

tions, polish, and edge-rounding to help identify the area of an artifact that was used and the use-action. Use-wear was not used to identify specific use-materials beyond the level of hard/high silica vs. soft material (Fullagar 1991).

Thirty-eight of the forty-one artifacts examined exhibit some evidence of wear, and/or residues relating to hafting or use. The resulting range of residues includes plant tissue, hair and skin fragments, possible bone or antler, possible blood residues, and unknown films of additive residue with drying cracks (suggesting that the residue was in liquid form when applied). Use-wear includes polish, edge rounding and damage, and striations with multiple orientations related to both cutting and hafting (Hardy 2000, 2001).

Hafting residues are confined to the proximal third to half portion of the artifact, and are characterized as various colored additive residues, possibly mastic, with and without drying cracks, plant fibers, skin fragments, and wood fragments. Hafting wear likewise is confined to the proximal third to half of the artifact, and is described as parallel, perpendicular or oblique striae, abraded ridges, polish and light polish. Use-residues are confined to the distal portion of the artifact near or on the working edge, and include hair fragments, skin fragments, possible bone/antler fragments, various colored residues with drying cracks, and plant fragments. Use-wear is confined to the distal portion of the artifact near or on the working edge, and is described as parallel, oblique, and perpendicular striae, polish, and edge damage (Hardy 2000, 2001).

Although this analysis is on-going, there are some preliminary results. Twenty projectile points have been examined: one complete point, one resharpened point, one nearly complete distal section, one midsection and 16 bases of varying lengths. The complete projectile point displays additive hafting residue. The resharpened point shows hafting wear in the form of perpendicular striae, oblique striae resulting from use possibly as a knife, and a residual skin fragment. The distal section displays use-wear polish while the midsection exhibits

no identifiable wear or residues. Eleven of the projectile point bases examined reveal wear or residue that is functionally informative. The remaining five bases have some form of light polish, but its patterning and location does not provide conclusive functional evidence. Seventeen of the projectile points show evidence of hafting. This is indicated by the presence of striations or polish resulting from the hafting material and binding material residues (Hardy 2000, 2001).

The examination of seven complete and fragmentary bifaces revealed that all exhibit evidence of use. Six of them display additive residue films with drying cracks, while one does not. Plant fragments and a dark residue on one of the tools is interpreted as evidence of hafting, while two others display use-wear striations (Figure 27). The presence of hair fragments has been noted on two of the implements. One of these displays a residue, oblique striae, and a hair

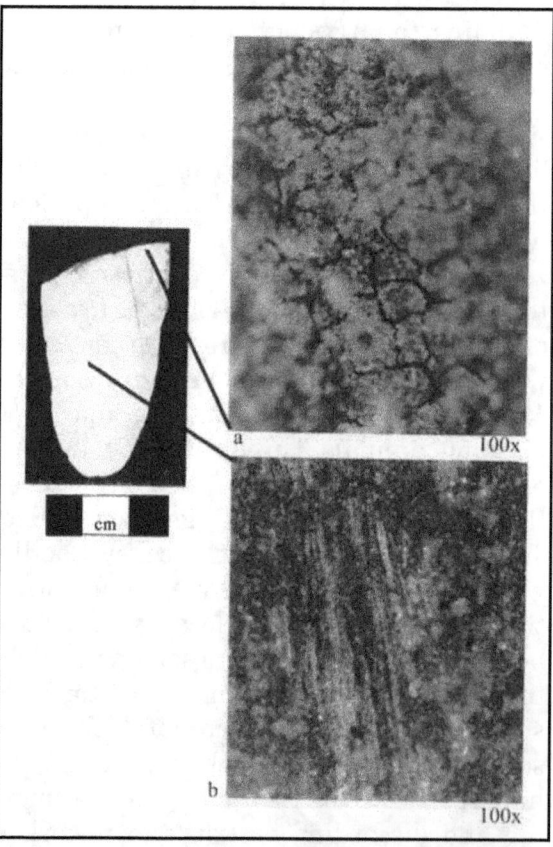

Figure 27. Example of residue with drying cracks (a) and use-wear striations (b) on Mesa biface. (Photo: B. Hardy)

with visible scales, suggesting it was used for cutting animal tissue. The use-wear on these artifacts is consistent with the assumed uses of this form of tool, that of a cutting implement. However it is impossible to determine if the tool was created as a knife, or if it was meant to be a lance point or other tool that was used for cutting.

Four gravers have been examined and three of them display evidence of use. One of these tools has some polish along one edge suggesting use as a whittling tool with the ventral surface in contact with the material being whittled or cut. Another graver has plant fragments adhering to the proximal end suggesting hafting, however, no use-residues or use-wear has been observed. A third graver has striations with multiple orientations suggesting utilization in complex cutting motions/activities, although the material it was used on is unknown (Hardy 2000, 2001). All of this evidence is consistent with graver use in the implement's assumed role as a multi-purpose tool.

Four retouched flakes have been examined and all display evidence of use. Microscopic examination of one of the flakes reveals that numerous fragments of a material that morphologically resembles bone or antler adhere along the edges of the flake and are associated with polish and striations, suggesting that the residue is related to use (Hardy 1994, 2000). Another flake exhibits a highly reflective residue with drying cracks associated with striations, edge damage, and polish. It appears to have been used on a hard or high silica content material. A third flake with two snap fractures displays multiple oblique striae suggesting that it broke while being used. The remaining flake exhibits an additive residue, parallel and oblique striae, polish and edge-rounding, suggesting use as a slicing or whittling tool (Hardy 2000, 2001). This type of use-wear is common on flakes more or less randomly selected, used as incidental tools (tools of the moment) and then discarded, and is consistent with assemblages from hunting-oriented sites (Judge 1973; Binford 1980).

The microscopic examination of four scrapers reveals that all of these tools re-

tain evidence of use. One of these tools exhibits polish so heavy along one of the working edges that it is visible macroscopically. This type of polish suggests that the tool was used to cut a hard or high silica material. Another scraper displays extensive heavy polish along the working edges and an imbedded hair fragment, suggesting a hide scraping action. A third specimen exhibits a black residue with drying cracks on the ventral surface and hair fragments imbedded in that residue, suggesting use as a hide scraper (Figure 28). The fourth scraper displays a reddish brown residue on the ventral surface and some striae perpendicular to the working edge. In an attempt to gain more information relating to the residue, this latter artifact was submitted to Microspec Analytical Group, Ltd., Holland, Michigan, for chemical analysis. A sample of the residue was examined using infrared spectroscopy. The results of this analysis were compared to known samples includ-

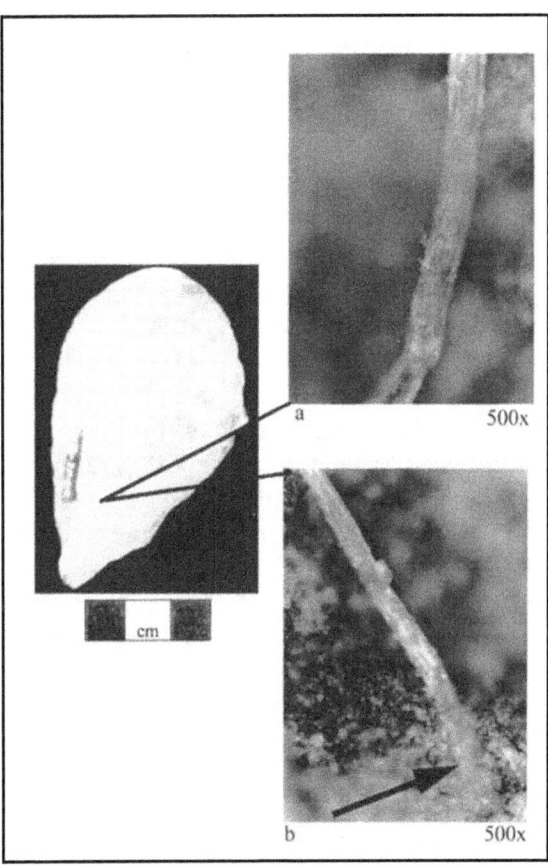

Figure 28. Mesa scraper fragment with hair (a), and hair embedded in residue (b). (Photo: B. Hardy)

ing two types of resin (pine and birch) and two modern flint flakes that were used to cut animal tissue, one on a Thompson's Gazelle and the other on a Wallaroo. The results did not yield a definitive identification, but the residue on the scraper more closely resembles the animal tissue residues than it does the resins (Hardy 2000, 2001). Further evaluation through chemical characterization of the residues might provide more information. With the exception of the first scraper described, the use-wear on all of the scrapers is consistent with the assumed hide-working function of scrapers. Three of these scrapers are associated with a hearth in the East Ridge Locality at which food preparation activities appear to have taken place. This was the only use area at the site where such activity occurred. The scraper with the use-wear, inferring work on a high silica or hard material, came from Locality Saddle.

During excavation in the East Ridge Locality, two large flat rocks (slabs) were found lying horizontally, adjacent to and protruding into the above-mentioned hearth feature. The rocks are manuports, and we assume that they were related to food preparation activities, perhaps functioning as a counter top does in a modern kitchen. Both rocks exhibit the same pattern of residues and wear. The superior (upper) surfaces are clean and flat. No use-residue or use-wear is present. The inferior (under) surfaces of the slabs are covered almost entirely by a brown-black stain, which under magnification exhibits drying cracks, and an occasional plant fiber (Hardy 2000, 2001). The rocks are limestone and the residue may be the result of the action of humic acids in the soil.

In general, the results of artifact use-wear and residue analysis are consistent with the activities the types of artifacts and their condition suggest took place atop the Mesa. Although use-wear and residue analysis of Mesa artifacts is on-going, there is no indication that additional work will provide evidence that will alter our view of the activities that were occurring at the Mesa between 11,700 and 9700 years BP.

PALEOECOLOGY
Subsistence Resources

The most compelling question raised by our research is why the Mesa was used as a hunting lookout. It is well established that caribou have been the primary human subsistence resource in arctic Alaska for millennia. Since the early 1900s, researchers have recognized that without caribou (which provide food, shelter, and material for tools and construction), or an animal of similar size, numbers, and habits, arctic Alaska would not be habitable by humans (Campbell 1968). Most recently this was demonstrated by a drastic crash in the arctic Alaska caribou population (Western Arctic Caribou Herd), beginning ca. 1890 and continuing through the 1920s. As a result, between 1900 and 1930 the Brooks Range, and all but the coastal region of the North Slope, were abandoned by the native population. It was not until the early 1930s, as caribou numbers began to increase, that people began living in the region once more (Gubser 1965; Simon Paneak, personal communication 1975).

Due to their numbers, gregarious nature and migratory habits, caribou can be successfully hunted without the aid of a vantage point of the Mesa's proportions. This is demonstrated by the rather nondescript location of numerous caribou hunting/kill sites throughout arctic Alaska (Gubser 1965; Binford 1978, 1980). Along the five-mile section of Iteriak Creek immediately north of the Mesa, there is a series of creekside archaeological sites. These sites represent use of the area from roughly 8000 years BP through the historic period. A number of these sites were used for caribou hunting activities, suggesting that the use of a vantage point of the Mesa's stature is not important in hunting caribou. This reality is further reinforced by the fact that none of the more recent cultural entities in the Iteriak Valley used the Mesa in any significant way. It is also worth noting that all of the other five known Mesa Complex sites are located on promontories commanding a field of view comparable to that of the type site, and at all of them there is little or no evidence of use by more recent cultures

(Reanier 1995; Ackerman 2001; Bever 2000).

These data suggest several possibilities: 1) the Mesa people were hunting caribou, but the population was extremely low, and a vantage point like the Mesa was needed to maximize procurement opportunities; 2) the Mesa people's primary prey species were not caribou, but animals whose habits required the use of a vantage point like the Mesa to conduct successful hunting operations; 3) all prey species in the region were low in numbers and no opportunity to obtain game animals could be overlooked. The common thread is that all these scenarios require hunting from a vantage point to make the best use of available game resources. The fact that the people that inhabited the region after ca. 7500 years BP did not utilize Mesa Complex site locales as hunting lookouts, suggests that the need to do so was a condition that was particular to the Pleistocene/Holocene transition period.

Climate and Vegetation

As previously mentioned, although the excavation of the Mesa has provided a tremendous amount of data regarding the lithic industry of its ancient occupants, and insights into their utilization of the site, it is not the kind of site that can provide much information concerning the past climate and ecology of the region. Any discussion concerning human history in arctic Alaska between ca. 12,000 and 10,000 years BP becomes one of how the environment affected prey species. Without that type of information it is impossible to begin to understand why the site was used as it was, or to gain insights into the life-ways of these early Alaskan residents. As a result we had to go afield to collect the paleoecological data that would help us develop a more complete picture of the terminal Pleistocene environment, and how it may have been exploited by the Paleoindians of the North Slope.[7] Daniel Mann conducted this aspect of research, and the following is a compilation of his results.

[7] We attempted DNA analysis of the bone fragments that were recovered from an East Ridge Locality hearth, hoping to identify the animal that had been the source of dinner. Due to the age of the bones and their burned condition, the extraction of a suitable DNA sample proved to be very difficult. The results of this work were tenuous at best, and suggested that the bones might be those of muskox (Pamela Groves, personal communication 2000). An effort to corroborate these findings at another laboratory proved unsuccessful (Elizabeth Shapiro, personal communication 2001).

Figure 29. Excavation in lake bed sediments at Lake of the Pleistocene. (Photo: M. Kunz)

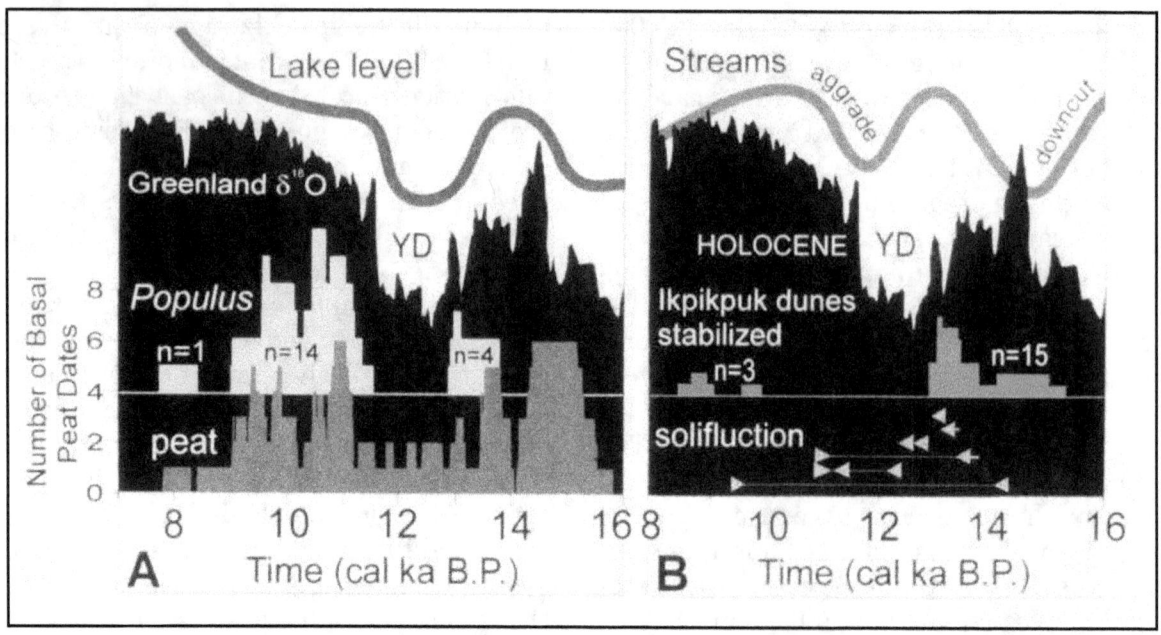

Figure 30. Synthesis of environmental changes in the Arctic Foothills during the Pleistocene-Holocene transition. Time scale in calendar years to allow comparison with Greenland $\delta^{18}O$ record from Grootes and Stuiver (1997). Lake levels inferred from stratigraphy at Lake of Pleistocene (LOP). A similar history for *Populus* emerges from LOP pollen data. Histograms depict numbers of ^{14}C dates whose calibrated 1 sigma age range falls within a given decade (YD= Younger Dryas). Dates on stabilization of the Ikpikpuk Dunes from Carter, 1993. (After Mann et al. 2002))

It would be difficult to find a time period containing more radical shifts in climate, vegetation, and biota than the several millennia spanning the Pleistocene to Holocene transition. Most intense was the period ca. 11,000 to 10,000 years BP, referred to as the Younger Dryas, a time when global climate jumped from interglacial conditions to glacial conditions, then back to interglacial conditions with decadal rapidity (Alley et al. 1993; Mayewski et al. 1993; Isarin and Bohncke 1999; Alley 2000). Widespread extinctions affected the world's megafauna during this interval (Martin and Klein 1984; Guthrie 1990). The flooding of Alaska's continental shelves, particulary after ca. 10,000 years BP, had significant impacts on climate, and vegetation changes repeatedly swept through arctic Alaska.

We used the stratigraphic archives in exposed geologic sections to infer how area soils, permafrost, and vegetation responded to these rapid climatic changes. Our primary resource are the deposits of the Lake of the Pleistocene (LOP), a drained lake that lies about 15 miles west of the Mesa (Figure 29).

The lake bottom sediments, which contain a record of lake level and vegetation changes through time, are exposed in a cutbank of the Etivluk River. These sediments extend back to the last interstadial, ca. 45,000 years BP, and their stratigraphic profiles were used to determine lake level fluctuations, as well as providing pollen and spores to reconstruct vegetation history (Figure 30). The evolution of paludification (development of peat) was determined by dating basal peats recovered through core augering the tundra. Floodplain dynamics were described by studying the chronology of terrace aggradation and erosion of area streams, and the history of solifluction was documented in exposed stratigraphic sections in the region (Mann et al. 2001, 2002).

Our research, and that of others, indicates that during full glacial times the exposed area of the land bridge (continental shelves), plus the permanently frozen Arctic ocean, produced an extreme continental climate over the Beringian land mass. The atmosphere was very dry, clouds were rare, and there was little precipitation during winter or summer. Until about 13,500 years BP, a full glacial landscape was present in the region surrounding the Mesa (Mann et al. 2001, 2002). That landscape has been referred to as steppe-tundra or mammoth-steppe (Guthrie 1990). There is no modern analog for this ecosystem, but it can best be described as a mosaic grassland, a sort of arctic prairie that supported a variety of grazing animals including mammoth, horse, and bison. The winters in the region were a few degrees colder and probably a bit windier than they are today, but with little cloud cover and much less snowfall. Compared to today, the summers were sunnier, warmer, a little windier, and much drier. All the conditions for grass to flourish were present. Most of the summer precipitation occurred during the late spring/early summer when it was most needed by the emerging vegetation. Solar radiation rapidly warmed a surface poorly insulated by grass. This quickly thawed an extensive active layer, which caused the permafrost level to remain fairly deep, and soil temperature to be warmer than it is today. Annually, the surface was kept in a disturbed state due to the aeolian deposition of loess and animal trampling. These factors, coupled with a high rate of evapotranspiration, promoted good surface drainage, and limited the amount of standing water (Kunz 1996).

Our data indicates that fluctuating moisture is the common theme in the paleoenvironmental records of the region. Water level changes in LOP coincide with changes in key landscape processes involving vegetation, organic-matter accumulation, flood plain dynamics, solifluction, and coastal plain sand dune activity. Some time in the millennia prior to 12,500 years BP, during the Bolling Chronozone — a period when the annual temperature was a few degrees warmer than today — more frequent rains accompanying a warmer climate were likely the cause for the initiation of paludification (peat development and buildup). Very rapid alluviation of valleys from at least 12,200 to 11,000 years BP, suggests a marked increase in hillslope erosion. This would have entailed increased summer rainfall, and/or increased thermokarst activity — the slumping caused by the melting of ice-rich permafrost. Coastal plain dunes were stabilized between 12,500 and 11,000 years BP probably as the result of increased soil moisture (Kunz et al. 1999a).

During the Younger Dryas and the return of a full glacial climate, decreased precipitation caused lake levels to fall, sand dunes to reactivate, and paludification to slow[8]. Streams downcut, probably because channel erosion by snow-melt floods continued, while the input of slope sediments from summer rains and/or thermokarst declined. Regional disappearance of scattered poplar refugiums may have been partly due to shrinkage of their flood plain habitat as streams entrenched (Kunz et al. 1999a).

The close of the Younger Dryas, some time between 10,000 and 9700 years BP, reinitiated the global warming trend, and once again annual temperatures climbed a few degrees higher than today. Water level in LOP rose, and poplars again expanded north of present latitudinal treeline. A brief episode of widespread solifluction probably occurred when thickening active layers released water stored in ice lenses below the thin active layers established during the Younger Dryas. After 10,000 years BP, denudation of slopes caused by increased summer rains, widespread solifluction, and probably increased thermokarst activity, again triggered rapid alluviation in valleys. Paludification was stimulated by increasing effective moisture by about 10,000 years BP. The spread of organic horizons would have caused active layers to thin and soil erosion to decline, initiating a long-term trend of entrenchment by the streams. As flood plains narrowed, loess deposition in downwind areas declined, probably enhancing soil acidification and further paludification (Kunz et al. 1999a).

This change is most graphically represented by the pollen recovered from the LOP sediments (Figure 31). Before 10,000 years BP, the species indicative of steppe-tundra

8 Although the annual temperature decreased to the full glacial level during the Younger Dryas, there was open water at least seasonally in the Arctic Ocean, and therefore more atmospheric moisture available (resulting in more precipitation) than in full glacial times.

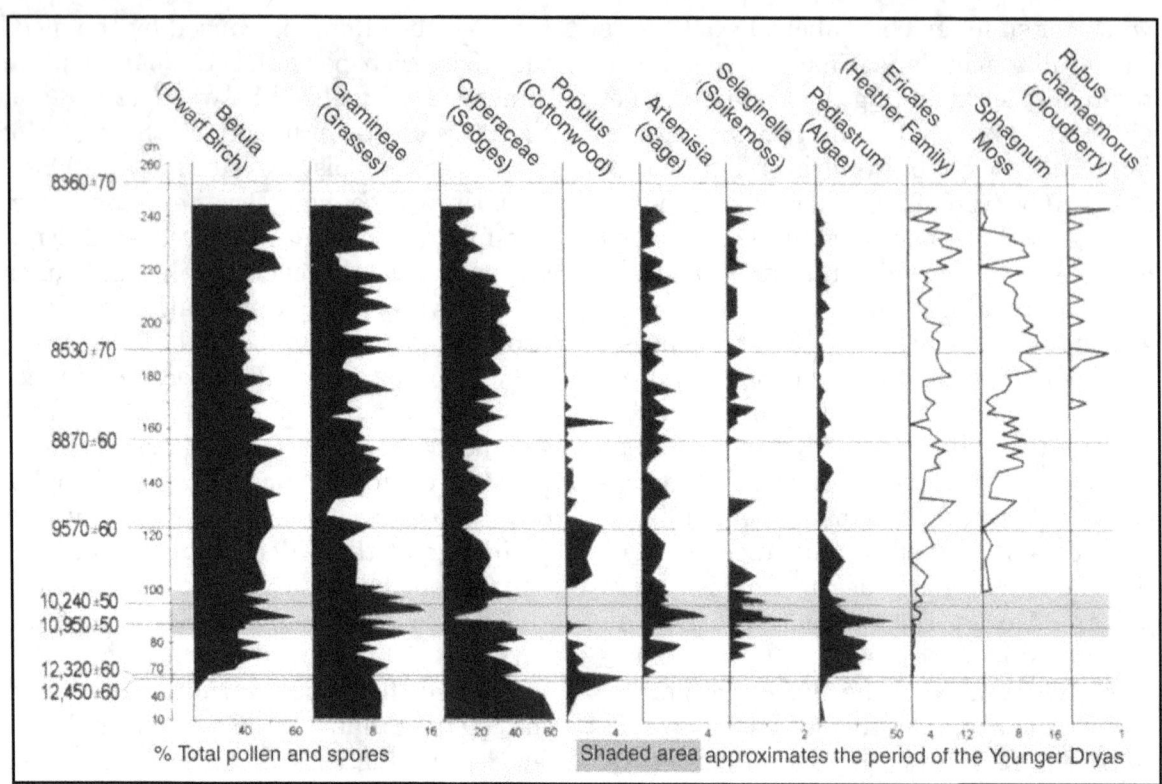

Figure 31. Percentage pollen and spore diagram from Lake of the Pleistocene. White curves show taxa associated with paludification. (After Mann et al. 2002)

are much more prevalent, and the species indicative of tussock-tundra are essentially absent. After 10,000 years BP, steppe-tundra species decrease, and tussock tundra species increase rapidly.

By 15,000 years BP, at least a portion of the Arctic Ocean was seasonally ice-free, and water from the Bering Sea was encroaching from the south. Over the next several thousand years, the geographical integrity of the Beringian subcontinent was compromised, and the severe continental climate moderated. More atmospheric moisture produced increasing cloud cover and precipitation. The winters became slightly warmer with more snow. The ground was covered with snow earlier in the year, and the annual spring breakup occurred later and produced more water. This caused the summers to be shorter in duration (fewer snow-free days and later green-up) and cooler with more precipitation. The cloudier summer skies reduced solar radiation and soil temperatures dropped, causing the active layer to shrink and the permafrost level to rise. This, coupled with a decreased rate

of evapotranspiration, dramatically added to the amount of surface water, providing for an increase in the mosquito population. More water meant fewer river bars were exposed and less loess available to be deposited over the landscape. This resulted in a more stable surface, reducing the available grass habitat. The cooler, wetter conditions favored the proliferation of tussock-tundra plant communities, and the build up of peat at the expense of grass (Kunz et al. 1999a).

Paleobiology

The fact that there was a lot of grass on Alaska's North Slope during the last glacial episode, is corroborated by the variety of grazers that inhabited the region during the late Pleistocene. The fossil remains of these animals have been preserved in the frozen loess and peat of the region. Annual high water events, such as spring breakup and river erosion, often expose their remains. As a result, the banks and gravel bars of the meandering rivers of the region have provided us with a collection of nearly

3000 fossil specimens — valuable data regarding species variety and density for the region during the late Pleistocene. The collection and analysis of this material by Paul Matheus has provided some unexpected results.

Early in the project, preliminary radiocarbon assays of bone collagen from these specimens indicated that horse and mammoth, although extremely numerous prior to and immediately following the last glacial maximum, were either absent from the region during the period of Mesa occupation, or that their numbers were so low they did not show up in the fossil record for that time period. Therefore, they could not have been a reliable subsistence resource for the human inhabitants of the region (Kunz 1996). As a result, we confined our research efforts to the large Pleistocene mammal species, bison, muskox[9], and caribou, that were represented in the fossil record as present in the region between ca. 12,000 and 10,000 years BP, and could have served as subsistence resources for the early inhabitants of arctic Alaska. However, the fact that horse and mammoth decline shortly after the last glacial maximum, and bison, muskox, and caribou do not, sheds some light on the ecosystem changes that were occurring at that time.

There were basically two types of grazers inhabiting arctic Alaska during the late Pleistocene: ruminants, such as bison, muskox, and caribou, and monogastrics such as mammoth and horse. These two grazer types have different foraging strategies that result from differences in their digestive anatomy, and as Guthrie (1982) has pointed out, because of this they are excellent paleoenvironmental indicators. Ruminants have evolved to thrive on diets of moderate-quality, low-fiber plant material. They have a slow gut-transit time which allows the animal to extract and absorb the maximum amount of energy and nutrition from a given forage. However, in order to gain enough protein and energy to successfully reproduce, ruminants require seasonal spikes in forage quality, e.g. a green-up season. Monogastrics on the other hand, have evolved to make the most of low-quality, high-fiber forage through a combination of rapid gut-transit time and a selective fermentation chamber called the caecum. However, forage passes so quickly through the gut of a monogastric, that protein and micro nutrients often are not efficiently extracted. Therefore, monogastrics must have a diet more diverse than ruminants (Matheus 1998, 2000; Kunz et al. 1999b). Because monogastric populations appear to have been affected long before ruminant populations in arctic Alaska, it may indicate that plant diversity in the region began decreasing following the last glacial maximum, and that the initial change was a decrease in grasses.

Our research indicates that caribou, which are by far the most numerous large mammal species through Holocene and recent times, appear to have been less abundant during the late Pleistocene, although they appear to be relatively common prior to and immediately following the last glacial maximum (Figure 32). While their reduced numbers may have been the result of competition with other species in a situation of rapidly changing habitat, their historically documented tendency for extreme (and unexplained) population fluctuations was probably an important factor as well. As a component of the late Pleistocene large herbivore community in arctic Alaska, caribou appear to have accounted for about 15% of individuals, while in recent times they account for more than 90%. It is well documented that from a subsistence point of view, biomass is a more meaningful measure than number of individuals, and our data indicate that during the late Pleistocene caribou accounted for only about 3% of the regional biomass. In recent times, their regional biomass level has been around 90% (Matheus 2000). A survey of archaeological sites in the region which have produced radiocarbon dates on culturally altered caribou bone, suggest that caribou

---

[9] Our muskox research is not yet complete. However, because of their non-migratory nature, social habits, and numbers (as well as negative archaeological evidence for their use as a prey animal) they are not generally considered to have been a primary subsistence resource in arctic Alaska; rather like moose, they appear to have been more a target of opportunity.

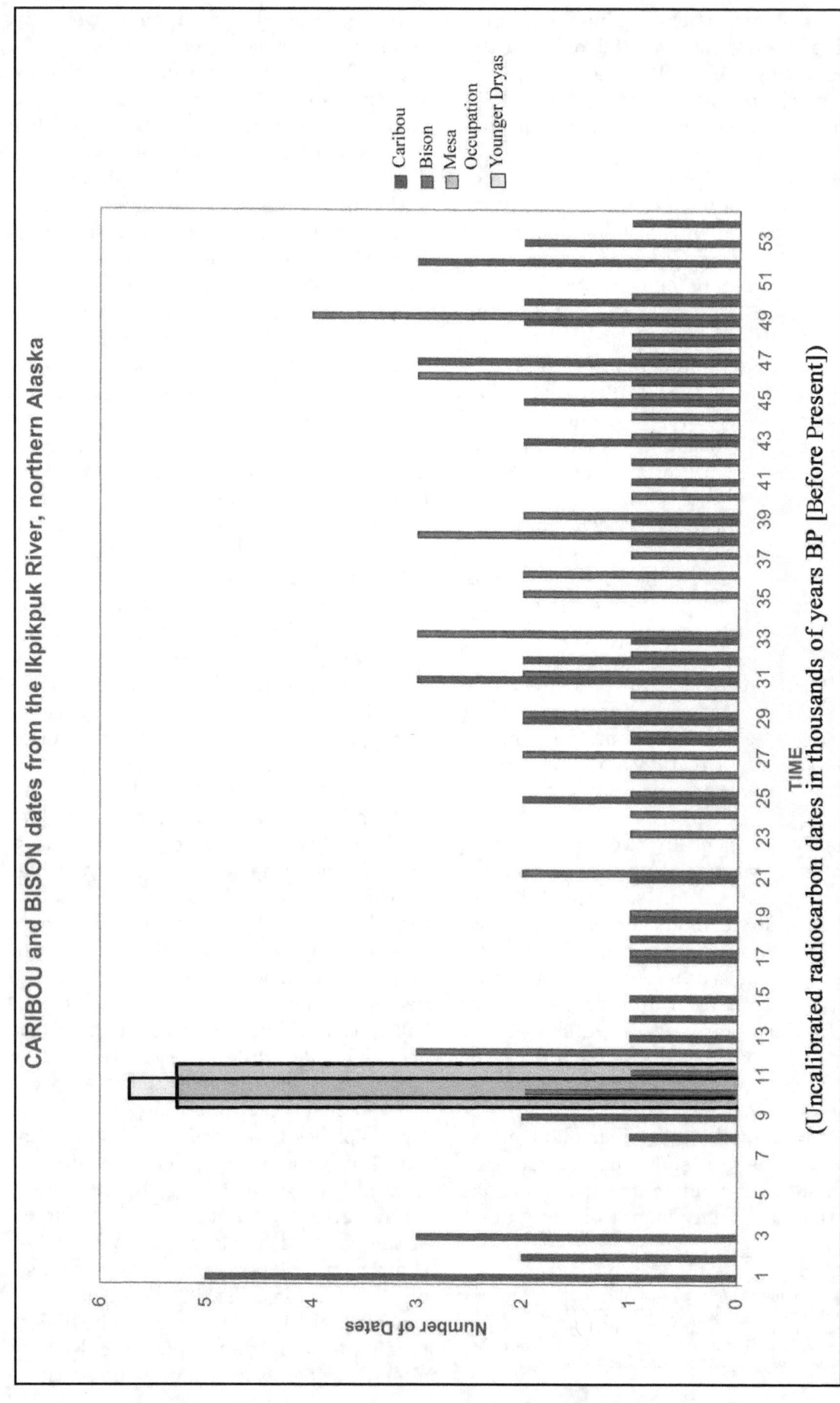

Figure 32.. Caribou and bison dates from the Ikpikpuk River, arctic Alaska, illustrating a relative absence of caribou during the time of the Younger Dryas episode and period of Mesa occupation. (Graph: C.M. Adkins)

numbers were not high enough for them to be a reliable subsistence resource much before 7500 years BP, by which time the regional landscape had become dominated by tussock-tundra (Kunz et al. 1999a).

By comparison, the percent of individuals for bison and muskox in the region during the late Pleistocene is 21% and 25% respectively. In terms of biomass, bison remains around 21%, while muskox drops to 9%, suggesting that muskox could not have served as a primary subsistence species. At present there are no bison in the region, and muskox are represented by an introduced population that represents less than 1% of the individual and biomass total for the current regional large herbivore population.

Bison became extinct in arctic Alaska at the end of the Pleistocene, and although muskox successfully made the transition into the Holocene and recent times, their remains are practically non-existent in the North Slope archaeological record. This evidence would seem to indicate that throughout the history of human presence on the North Slope, muskox have never been a significant subsistence resource. As a result, although we have no archaeological evidence demonstrating an association between terminal Pleistocene humans and bison, we believe that bison were the most likely prey species of the Mesa Paleoindians. Among other evidence, we base this conclusion on the data from 50 AMS radiocarbon assays of fossil bison bones recovered from the Ikpikpuk River, 60 miles north of the Mesa, which show that bison were present in the region while the Mesa was occupied (Matheus 1998, 2000). It is worth noting that at the same time, caribou numbers appear to be so low that they are absent from the fossil record, and probably are not a reliable subsistence resource (Figure 32). We suspect that by 10,500 years BP, the bison population was greatly reduced — although they were probably more numerous than other large herbivore species such as caribou and muskox — and by themselves may not have been able to sustain the human population. This suggests that the less numerous species may have been a more important resource than previously realized.

As a result of these circumstances, arctic Paleoindians may have been even more dependent upon bison than their southern relatives on the North American High Plains. While the Mesa Paleoindians possessed a lithic technology that appears to be based upon a bison economy identical to that of the southern Paleoindians, the arctic bison and ecosystem were significantly different from that of the High Plains. These differences provide valuable insights into the life-ways of the Mesa Paleoindians.

Bison priscus was the only bison present in Alaska until the terminal Pleistocene. About 400,000 years ago *B. priscus* entered North America from Asia, passing through Alaska on its way to the North American plains. On the plains it appears to have evolved into the famous long-horned *B. latifrons*, which in turn is believed to have given rise to *B. antiquus* (Guthrie 1990). In Alaska, *B. priscus* remained unchanged. Around 12,000 years BP, a smaller short-horned bison, *B. occidentalis,* appears in Alaska and shortly thereafter is present on the High Plains (Guthrie 1990). It appears that *B. occidentalis* is the progenitor of modern bison. Our data do not tell us if *B. priscus* and *B. occidentalis* are contemporaries in Alaska, or if *B. occidentalis* is nothing more than a diminution of *B. priscus*, the result of ecological stress generated by the terminal Pleistocene environmental changes. Our faunal collection contains hundreds of bones of mature bison, and the range of size for any given bone is extreme. However, there is no temporal constraint associated with the size variations, so they could reflect either sexual dimorphism or speciation. The bottom line is that there is no way to determine if the bison on the North Slope, at the time the Mesa was occupied, were the huge *B. priscus* or the smaller, yet large by modern standards, *B. occidentalis*.

Since almost all data concerning interaction between humans and bison in North America comes from the Great Plains, these data may not be universally applicable to the North Slope. Although the dentition of *B. priscus,* as well as plant fragments found in the teeth of frozen fossil specimens indicate that *B. priscus* was a grazing specialist, there is also data (Guthrie 1990) that suggest that browsing could account for up to 50% of foraging activity if the range was grass-poor. As discussed previously, the terminal Pleistocene range on the North Slope appears to have been grass-poor, and therefore foraging and other bison behavior, whether *B. priscus* or *B. occidentalis*, may have been somewhat atypical when compared to their southern relatives.

In the temperate latitudes, bison migrate primarily as a response to the seasonal south to north greenup of their range. In arctic Alaska the timing and pattern of greenup is not south to north, but is more influenced by topography, primarily slope and slope aspect. This is because the exposure of the surface to solar radiation is so critical to the emergence and growth of vegetation. South facing slopes green up first, while slopes with northern exposures green up last. This suggests that bison in the vicinity of the Mesa would have had access to nutritious forage nearly all spring and summer by just going around to the other side of the hill, rather than having to migrate any real distance (Kunz et al. 1999b).

In general, nonmigratory herbivores are larger than those that migrate, and *B. priscus* was large. Another reason that *B.*

priscus may have retained its large size in the Arctic, is that large ruminants are far more efficient at digesting poor quality forage than are small ruminants (Guthrie 1990). Also worthy of note is that limited sexual dimorphism is usually found in species that are seasonally migratory, because they live most of the year in a mixed herd, and competitiveness would be a negative strategy. As a species, *B. priscus* is very sexually dimorphic, the males being considerably larger than the females. This suggests that most of the year the males and females lived in separate bands in order to reduce agonistic behavior (Guthrie 1990). These data suggest that in arctic Alaska, *B. priscus* (and probably *B. occidentalis*) likely congregated in small bands scattered across the landscape, in predictable locales, and were not migratory in the true sense. Because their group size was small, and their behavior rather sedentary, the methods the Mesa Paleoindians used to hunt them were probably somewhat different than the methods employed by hunters on the High Plains (Kunz et al. 1999a). Nonetheless, if the residents of the Mesa were hunting *Bison priscus*, it must have been quite an adventure.

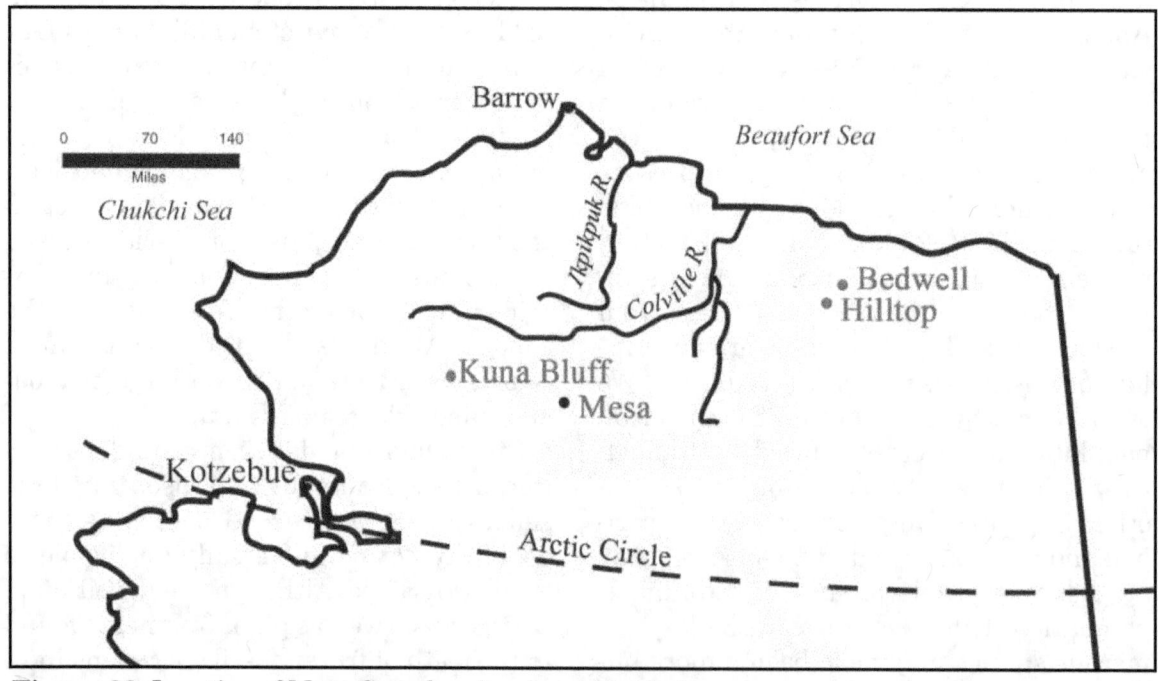

Figure 33. Location of Mesa Complex sites in arctic Alaska.

IMPLICATIONS OF THE MESA COMPLEX FOR NORTH AMERICAN ARCHAEOLOGY AND THE PEOPLING OF THE NEW WORLD

Research at the Mesa, Hilltop, Bedwell, and Kuna Bluff Mesa Complex sites (Figure 33) in arctic Alaska, as well as recent work in Siberia and South America, demonstrates a need to reexamine both the traditional model of migration into the New World, and the notion of a Beringian origin for Paleoindian culture/technology, (Kunz and Reanier 1994, 1995; Reanier 1995; Slobodin and King 1996; Dillehay 1997; Kunz 2001a). Some interesting points bear on this need. Core and blade technology is a primary aspect of late Pleistocene Western Beringian (Siberian) archaeological assemblages. Eastern Beringian (Alaskan) blade and microblade complexes are quite similar, and seem firmly grounded in Siberian traditions. In contrast, there is a contemporaneous classic Paleoindian presence in Eastern Beringia that is completely New World in character, and directly related to the High Plains Paleoindian cultures. These circumstances suggest that the Pleistocene cultural landscape of the North American Arctic may be much more complex than originally thought, and that the region could well be the birthplace of the Paleoindian tradition.

Migrations

The key to successful settlement of a region by any mammalian species including human, is being able to maintain a biologically viable population. This can be accomplished by having a birth and growth-to-maturity rate that is greater than the death rate, and/or a regular or periodic recharge of the immigrant population from their home territory. The bottom line is one of numbers. It is unlikely that with late Pleistocene technology it would be possible for a group of people to cross open ocean and arrive together on the shores of North or South America in numbers sufficient for successful settlement (Straus 2000; Kunz 2001a). However there is little doubt that watercraft were important, probably even critical, to the initial colonization and subsequent expansion of humans throughout the New World. While open ocean travel over great distances probably was not within the capabilities of late Pleistocene humans, coastal and near-shore travel was. This suggests that the progenitors of the Paleoindians were from northern and eastern Asia, and that the route they followed was essentially terrestrial.

The fact that the dry-land connection between Asia and North America was useable, is evidenced by the fact that the Ice Age faunal assemblages of Siberia and Alaska are of almost identical composition (Guthrie 1982). If groups of animals could successfully cross, re-cross, get their populations recharged, establish viable populations, and achieve successful settlement via the land bridge, then so could humans. All things considered, it seems to be the only way that the indigenous human population of the New World could have become that which is reflected in the archaeological record of 11,500 years BP.

Around 15,000 years BP, the land bridge and Eastern Beringia were probably witnessing the arrival of culturally distinct groups from across northern and eastern Asia. Given the positions of the continental glaciers at that time, it is unlikely that people could have moved south out of Alaska by land or water (Mandryk et al. 1998) (Figure 34). These groups may have been contained in Beringia for a millennia or so, some probably blending and developing new cultural identities and technologies in response to the changing environmental conditions. At the same time, some groups may have remained generally unchanged in terms of the cultural and technological orientation they had brought with them from Western Beringia.

Although currently some credence is given to the possibility of human migrations from Pleistocene Europe to North America along or via North Atlantic sea ice margins, it remains generally accepted that the primary source of New World human population were the indigenees of Western Beringia/Northern Asia (Straus 2000). However the when, how, and cultural composition of the migration(s) may be considerably different than the long-accepted model. Evidence suggests that a coastal migration route out of the Arctic after 14,000 years BP model, is at least as viable as an ice-free corridor model (Mann and Hamilton 1995). The key however, whether by land or by sea, is the Arctic itself and the ability of humans to survive there.

The technology that allowed humans to live in the Arctic also provided the where-with-all for the manufacture of reliable, seaworthy watercraft. Under reasonable conditions, people utilizing watercraft can transport more goods and cover distances faster, than can people engaged in pedestrian travel. If both modes of travel were used by groups migrating out of the Arctic across the Western Hemisphere, it is not surprising that there would be a differential rate of expansion. It is quite likely that this occurred, and that different cultural groups with different environmental orientations were involved.

Technology vs. Environment

While the large, cold-adapted fauna of northern North America and Siberia roamed across the land bridge throughout the Pleistocene, the subarctic and Arctic served as a filter, screening out humans until their technology was sufficient to allow them to live in such climes. The technical breakthrough that allowed humans to live in the Arctic/subarctic was the invention of the eyed needle, and the subsequent development of a sophisticated sewing technology (Kunz 1997). The earliest indications of the existence of eyed needles occur in the archaeological records of the trans-Baikal and northern Mongolia around 30,000 years BP (Troeng 1993; Sergey Vasil'ev, personal communication 2002). By contrast, the oldest archaeological sites on the Siberian margin of the land bridge appear to date around 15,000 years BP. If so, this evidence suggests that it took roughly 15,000 years for humans to disperse to the limits of western Beringia while developing a sewing technology sophisticated enough to produce tailored,

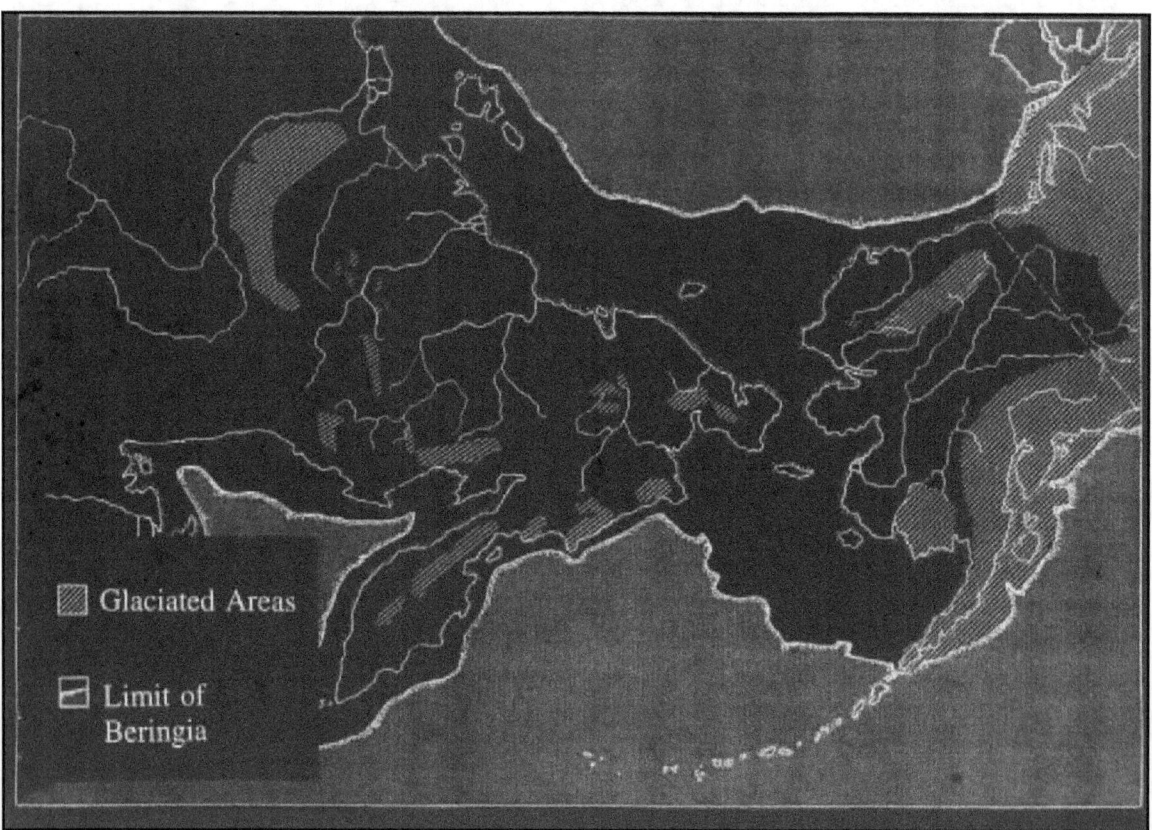

Figure 34. Extent of glaciation in Beringia about 15,000 BP. (Map: M. King)

weather-tight — and in some cases water-tight — clothing and shelter sufficient to allow year-round occupation of sub-Arctic and Arctic environments. Based on this evidence it seems reasonable to assume that no viable human populations were present in the Western Hemisphere prior to ca. 15,000 years BP.

North American Pleistocene Cultures

Nenana

It is worth noting that almost as soon as the Pleistocene presence of humans in the North American plains was proven (Figgins 1927), researchers began looking to the Arctic for older evidence (Nelson 1935, 1937; de Laguna 1936). What they found was not the lanceolate projectile point/bifacial reduction industry of the classic Paleoindian assemblages of the High Plains, but core and blade complexes typical of Siberian Upper Paleolithic cultures. While isolated finds of projectile points morphologically similar to the distinctive lanceolate Paleoindian points of the North American High Plains and Southwest were encountered and/or reported (Collins 1937; Rainey 1939, 1940), no sites in which these supposed Paleoindian artifacts made up a legitimate assemblage component were located.

Until recently all of the known terminal Pleistocene-age lithic industries of Eastern Beringia included core and blade reduction in their assemblages, as do all of the Western Beringian lithic industries of the upper Paleolithic (Dumond 1980; West 1981; Anderson 1988). An important aspect of these assemblages is the reduction of a cobble or chunk of stone to a core, which is designed to repetitively produce spalls/blades of regularized dimensions. Often formal tools are made on or from blades, as are the incidental tools, since much of the debitage consists of failed blades.

Based on manufacturing techniques, tool types and forms, the Nenana Complex of Interior Alaska exhibits a strong Siberian flavor. Projectile points, manufactured through bifacial reduction of cobbles or flakes, occur in Nenana assemblages as they do in late Pleistocene Siberian industries

(Dikov 1996). However, there is no morphological or stylistic consistency among the lanceolate forms. The artifact form that is diagnostic of the Nenana Complex is a small, triangular or teardrop-shaped biface, usually made on a thin flake, and often poorly and incompletely flaked (Goebel et al. 1991; Hoffecker 2001). As with the Siberian sites of the late Pleistocene, microblade technology also appears to be part of the Nenana assemblage, and is a major component of its cultural derivative, the Denali Complex (Holmes 2001). The Siberian influence in interior Alaska is demonstrated by the continuous presence of microblade technology from the earliest times, ca. 11,800 years BP, until less than 1200 years BP (Mobley 1991; Bever 2000). Evidence for the geographic extent of this influence is essentially unbroken as far south as British Columbia, appearing there shortly before mid-Holocene times (Clark 2001).

Paleoindian

The Paleoindian tradition was defined in the decades immediately following the 1926 Folsom discovery and the 1932 Clovis discovery at Blackwater Draw in New Mexico. During those years the term Paleoindian came to be associated with a specific cultural tradition, rather than just a time period, because it was recognized that most North American terminal Pleistocene-age sites shared common attributes. The stone tools and other cultural materials in these sites were often found in association with the remains of Pleistocene megafauna. The artifact assemblage from these sites displayed a uniformity in manufacturing technology, so that the type, style, and morphology of the tools, especially the projectile points, were similar from site to site[10].

The cornerstone of Paleoindian lithic tech-

[10] The original excavations at Blackwater Draw demonstrated that Clovis was found in the lowest cultural strata of the site associated with mammoth and bison remains and that Folsom lay directly above Clovis and was associated only with bison. These circumstances demonstrated that Clovis was older than Folsom and that Clovis and Folsom were the two oldest cultures of the emerging Paleoindian tradition. Fluting is a distinctive way of thinning the base of a projectile point and is characteristic of both Clovis and Folsom projectile points. Fluting is not a characteristic of projectile points of the more recent Paleoindian cultures. As a result, fluting (fluted projectile points) has become an indicator of great antiquity.

nology is bifacial reduction, which the Paleoindians took to one of its highest technological levels. Bifacial stone tools, such as projectile points or knives, are manufactured through the reduction of a cobble, chunk, or large flake down to the finished implement. The other tools in Paleoindian assemblages, primarily the incidental tools, such as spokeshaves, drills and gravers are made from/on amorphous flakes, the detrital by-products of the reduction process. It was by these criteria that the Paleoindian tradition was described and defined. For those who have worked with these classic Paleoindian materials, the term Paleoindian evokes a mental picture of large, uniformly well made lanceolate points associated with a specific assemblage of tools and debitage.

Over the years the term Paleoindian became synonymous with the first inhabitants or oldest cultures in the New World. It must be remembered that this perception developed as the Paleoindian tradition was being defined, a time when no other serious contenders for the position of earliest New World inhabitants had been recognized. Generally speaking that perception continues today, except that now there may be a serious contender or two to consider. Nonetheless, the lanceolate projectile points of the classic North American Paleoindian cultures remain the hallmark for the earliest geographically extensive, technologically distinct, cultural tradition in the Western Hemisphere.

The original criteria used to define the Paleoindian tradition have stood the test of time, and have proven to be culturally valid (Irwin and Wormington 1970; Judge 1973; Frison 1978, 1988; Lynch 1991). Any archaeological assemblage which can meet those criteria can be termed Paleoindian. By the same measure, the term Paleoindian cannot be applied to terminal Pleistocene assemblages that meet the age criteria but not the techno/cultural criteria. To do so is to ignore the basic constructs of archaeology.

Alaska's Mesa Complex fulfills all of the Paleoindian criteria, whereas none of the other terminal Pleistocene Alaskan complexes do (Powers and Hoffecker 1989;

Goebel et al. 1991; Holmes 1996; Hoffecker 2001; Holmes 2001). This distinction is not made to detract from the importance of the non-Paleoindian assemblages; in fact, just the opposite. It is done from the perspective of being able to compare different archaeological cultures.

Fluted Points in Eastern Beringia

In the late 1960s, investigations at the Batza Téna obsidian source in interior Alaska revealed several sites that contained fluted lanceolate points in sufficient numbers to consider them a possible assemblage component (Clark and Clark 1975, 1983, 1993; Clark 1991). Unfortunately, no dateable material was associated with the excavated artifacts, and obsidian hydration dates on the points ranged over thousands of years, rendering age determinations inconclusive.

Research indicates that Alaskan fluted projectile points are technologically distinct from Clovis and Folsom points (Clark 1991; Reanier 1995). In general, Alaskan fluted point technology most closely resembles that of Folsom, yet remains distinct due to its technological inconsistency and stylistic variability. At some Alaskan sites there appears to be a strong association between fluted points and microblade technology (Bowers 1982; Clark and Clark 1983; Reanier 1995; Bever 2000). This is not surprising, as the techniques used to set up and strike blades/microblades from a core are closely allied to the techniques employed in fluting.

These circumstances suggest (except as discussed later) that in general, Alaskan fluted points are not part of the lineage of Paleoindian technological evolution that is evident in temperate North America. If, as we suspect, most Alaskan fluted points are the result of isolated independent invention, there is no cultural link between them and the classic Paleoindian cultures. While less probable, it is possible that the Alaskan fluted points represent a cultural backwash from the High Plains — perhaps resulting from Folsom people following a disappearing ecosystem northward. In that case there is a cultural relationship, but not one of Alaskan primogeniture. Finally, we still do not know the age of most Alaskan fluted points; are they Pleistocene or Holocene or both? For now the genesis and temporal placement of most Alaskan fluted points remains unknown.

Mixing Technologies

In the other direction, while cores and blades do occur in some Paleoindian assemblages (primarily Clovis), their presence appears to be more site specific than tradition-wide (Bradley 1993). Most often when blades occur in Paleoindian assemblages, they seem to occur at quarry locations (Tony Baker, personal communication 2001). In non-quarry sites, the occurrence of blades is probably indicative of independent invention, rather than representing a link to Old World cultures (Sanger 1970). By the same measure, burins, which are a common tool in core and blade industries, are generally uncommon and stylistically different when they are present in Paleoindian and other bifacial systems (Bever 2000).

Typically, in the assemblages of the Western Beringian terminal Pleistocene cultures, there is a degree of melding between the two reduction systems (Dikov 1979; Slobodin and King 1996;). Blades and microblades are the primary or major components with tools such as incidental cutting, incising, scraping, and boring implements often made on or from them. Other tools, such as projectile points and knives, may be produced through bifacial reduction. Despite the infusion of bifacial elements, these complexes remain core and blade oriented. It is not surprising that the same circumstances prevail in the technologically related cultures of adjacent Eastern Beringia (Cook 1969; Powers and Hoffecker 1989; Holmes 1996).

Beginnings

In Eastern Beringia two distinct cultural

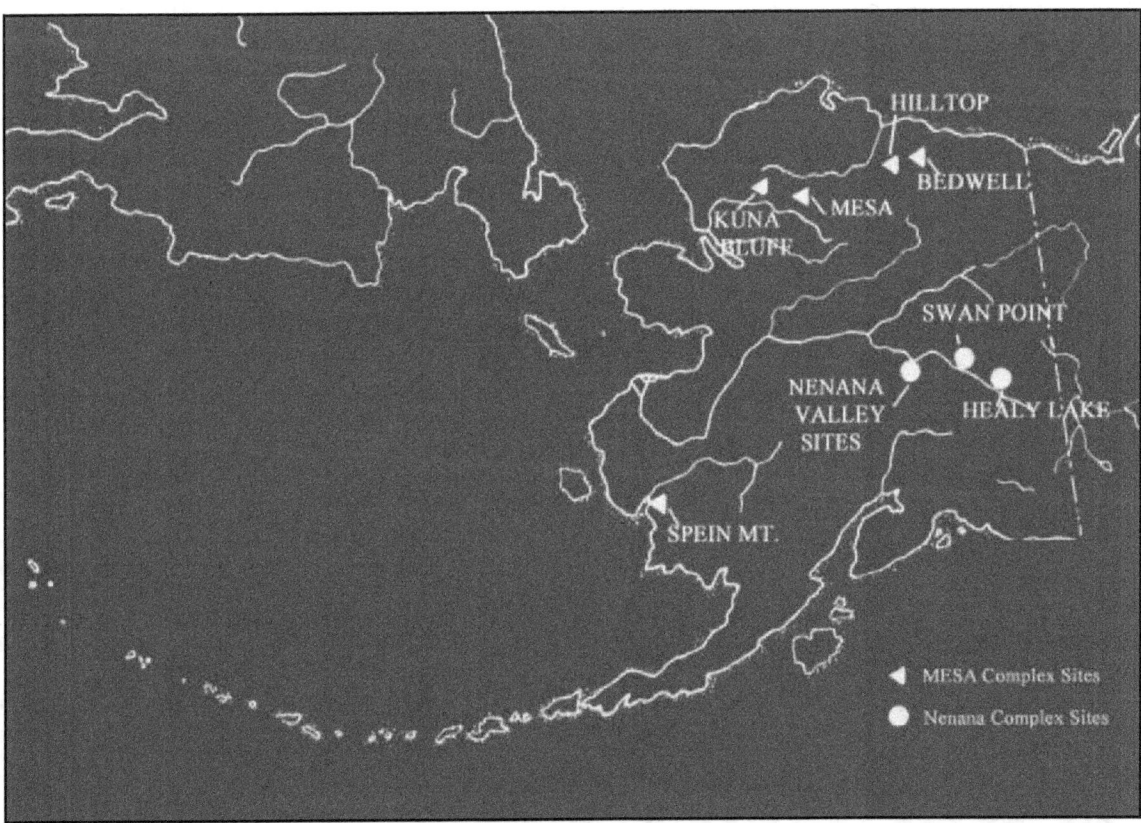

Figure 35. Location of Mesa and Nenana Complex sites in Alaska.

entities appear to be as old or older than Clovis: The Nenana Complex of interior Alaska and the Mesa Complex of arctic and western Alaska. (Figure 35). These complexes are not cultural isolates like other proposed "earliest" entities. The stone tool assemblages of Nenana and Mesa are replicated at a number of sites that are chronologically consistent across a large geographic area ((Powers and Hoffecker 1989; Goebel et al. 1991; Bever 2000; Hoffecker 2001). The Nenana Complex is Siberian in flavor, while the Mesa Complex is classic Paleoindian (Figure 36).

So how did this happen? Why are there two very different yet contemporaneous Pleistocene cultural complexes in arctic Alaska, and why are there classic Paleoindians in Alaska, more than 3000 miles from the North American High Plains, the heartland of Paleoindian activity? To shed light on this question requires a review of what is known about the oldest culture of the Paleoindian tradition, the Clovis Complex.

The archaeological discovery at Folsom, New Mexico in 1926 demonstrated that humans were present in the Western Hemisphere at the close of the Pleistocene (Cook 1927; Figgins 1927). Six years later at Blackwater Draw, the discovery of a lithic tool assemblage that lay stratigraphically below the Folsom level, suggested that humans had been present on the North American High Plains prior to the Folsom bison hunters (Howard 1936)

Over the next 50 years, as more discoveries were made, excavations undertaken, and radiocarbon age determinations became the dating standard, it was evident that Clovis was not only the most ancient of the Paleoindian complexes, but also the most geographically widespread. Clovis appears to radiate outward from a High Plains/Southwest concentration of "classic Clovis" morphology, to more loosely defined derivative forms found coast to coast from southern Canada to northern Mexico and beyond (Morrow and Morrow 1999).

While radiocarbon data from Clovis sites suggest that those sites in the Plains and Southwest may be slightly older than those found elsewhere, possibly because reliable dates from sites outside the High Plains are lacking, there is no clear indication as to where the complex originated. More importantly, there is no recognizable Clovis progenitor. This seems somewhat odd because the geographic extent, almost instantaneous geographic proliferation, and density of Clovis sites, suggest a progenitor should be visible in the archaeological record, represented by at least a few technologically similar sites.

Given the current archaeological data, it almost seems as though the Clovis culture spontaneously appeared in the High Plains and Southwest, and then spread rapidly in the form of regional derivatives throughout the rest of temperate North America (Anderson and Gillam 2000). However, aside from a good science fiction read, the creation of a cultural complex through spontaneous generation, is a difficult concept to grasp. As a

Figure 36. Comparison of Nenana and Mesa Complex assemblages respectively. (Photos: M. Bever, M. Kunz)

result, archaeologists have been searching for Clovis antecedents with crusader-like zeal and intensity, ever since there was enough data to suggest that there was no obvious precursor. Since cultural identity in the late Pleistocene archaeological record is based almost entirely on components of the lithic artifact assemblage, a degree of technological similarity would seem appropriate as a yardstick in the search for a Clovis progenitor.

While there have been a number of older-than-Clovis sites brought forward, few survive the scrutiny they receive. Nonetheless, there are a few sites that may indeed be older than Clovis, such as Monte Verde, Meadowcroft, and a few others (Adovasio and Carlisle 1982; Dillihay 1997). At present however, sites such as these appear to be one-of-a-kind occurrences which produce unique, and often meager artifact assemblages that are found nowhere else, and display no apparent technological relationship to Clovis. For those reasons alone, they seem unlikely candidates as a source for Clovis. Ultimately the Clovis progenitor must stem from an Old World population, because that is where modern humans evolved. How and where that population arrived in the Western Hemisphere obviously determines the rest of the story.

South from the Arctic

The presence of the Mesa Complex, a classic High Plains Paleoindian Complex in Eastern Beringia, more than 3000 miles from the Paleoindian heartland, must be either the result of a northward migration of High Plains Paleoindians, or a Paleoindian evolution that occurred in Beringia. What follows is somewhat speculative, but it is speculation resulting from converging data solidly derived from a variety of independent sources.

While it seems logical for people to migrate south from the Arctic toward a more temperate environment and ecosystems that are more easily exploited and provide a wider range of subsistence resources, the reverse, a journey from south to north, moving into progressively deteriorating conditions of climate, ecosystem diversity, and

mobility, seems illogical. Therefore, we think it is reasonable to view the Mesa Complex as the result of in-place cultural evolution and adaptation.

At 14,500 years BP, the Ushki 1 site on the Kamchatka Peninsula provides the earliest known date for human occupation of the Western Beringian margin of the land bridge[11] (Dikov 1996). On the Eastern Beringian margin, the Mesa at 11,700 years BP provides the earliest known date[12] (Kunz and Reanier 1994). With as little as 56 miles of land bridge lying between the two continental margins, it seems odd that the chronologies of Western and Eastern Beringian human occupation are divergent by almost 3000 years. The reason for this may have been that the land bridge proper was a good place to make a living. The area was extensive, about 320,000 square miles. The human population was probably quite small and scattered, so there was no real competition for resources and no pressure to move, other than for seasonal rounds. However, as has been pointed out by many other researchers, since it's all under water now, we've not yet discovered any direct evidence to support this assumption (Fladmark 1979; Easton 1992; Mann and Hamilton 1995).

While all prehistoric hunter/gatherer groups were opportunistic when it came to exploiting their environment, most had a basic economic orientation which was reflected in their tool kit. The High Plains Paleoindians were primarily bison hunters, and that is why the basic tool kit of the various High Plains Paleoindian cultures are so similar (Frison 1991; Sellet 1999, 2001).

---

[11] It should be noted that recent excavations at Ushki 5 located across a bay from Ushki 1, suggest that the oldest levels at Ushki 1 may be no older than ca. 11,500 BP. Nonetheless, given the information from other Western Beringian Sites, for the present it seems reasonable to assume that the 14,500 BP date from Ushki 1 represents the earliest occupation of the area (Sergei Slobodin, personal communication 2002).

---

[12] As previously discussed in the Chronology section, the authors can find no definitive evidence to discount the 11,700 BP date or the 11,200 BP date. Both of these dates are from the same hearth and are probably the same age but appear divergent due to the Younger Dryas effect. Data from the Tuluaq Hill site where AMS radiocarbon dates associated with Mesa Complex artifacts are dated at 11,200 BP, support our position.(Rasic 2000, personal communication 2001)

Along these lines, it is worth noting that an association between Mesa and Clovis may be seen in a comparison of the two lithic assemblages. This is most graphically demonstrated in the type B Mesa bifaces (see the typology/technology section) which are manufactured to the "finished" stage by the direct percussion technique. The removal of large flakes, often running across most or all of the face of the artifact, a biface thinning technique typical of Clovis, is relatively common. Some delicate pressure retouch along the edges completes the process. The Mesa projectile point manufacturing process also utilizes percussion flaking to perform much of the thinning and shaping work. The final stage shaping is achieved through very robust pressure flaking. This obliterates most of the evidence for the work that created the point's distinctive diamond, or lenticular, cross section. Additionally, a small percentage of Mesa Complex projectile points are fluted (Figure 37). In about half the examples, the fluting appears more incidental than purposeful, but some bases were undoubtedly thinned by intentional fluting. Given these similarities, it seems reasonable to entertain the idea that the Mesa and Clovis complexes may stem from a common Beringian ancestor.

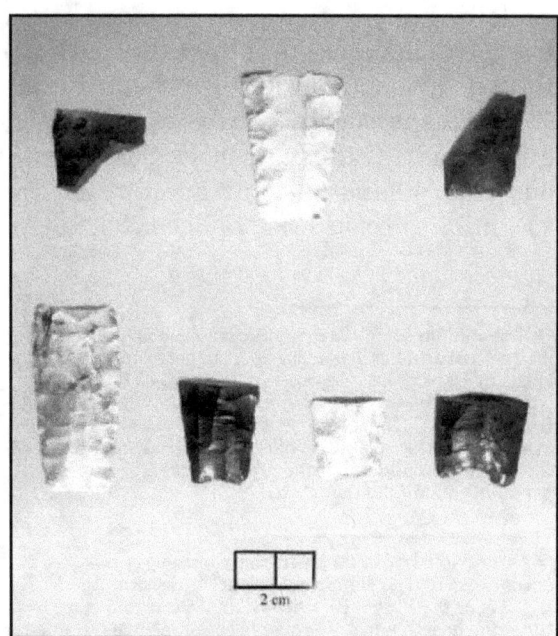

Figure 37. Evidence of fluting on Mesa projectile points. (Photo: M. Kunz)

In terms of subsistence resources, the terrestrial arctic ecosystem allows little latitude in exploitation (Hall 1961). It has been demonstrated that without the presence of a large, gregarious, migratory herd animal, humans cannot survive in the region (Campbell 1968). During the late Pleistocene, the two large herd mammals present in arctic Alaska were caribou and bison. It is possible that the rudiments of the Paleoindian culture and tool kit may have developed on the Bering land bridge between 15,000 and 14,000 years BP, as the result of a bison and caribou based economy.

By about 15,000 years BP, water was beginning to encroach upon the land bridge (Mann and Hamilton 1995). At the same time, increased precipitation was changing the vegetational composition of the region (Mann et al. 2002). As the land bridge was gradually inundated, both humans and animals were forced to the continental margins, providing the human population with two basic choices: survive on the failing resources of the mosaic habitat bordering the land bridge termini, or leave the region. In our scenario, exodus was the generally preferred choice, and groups probably started moving south via a coastal route by 14,000 years BP. Some time between 12,000 and 11,000 years BP, as the water continued to rise, the small population of Paleoindians that remained in the Arctic began to occupy the area that is today's coastal plain and foothills of arctic Alaska. This is the only region in Alaska where classic Paleoindian assemblages are found (Bever 2000).

During the last glacial maximum, ca. 22,000 years BP, the ice of the Alaska Peninsula Glacier Complex formed the southeast border of Beringia (Mann and Hamilton 1995). It separated the unglaciated coast stretching westward toward Siberia from the northwest coast of North America. At its maximum extent, the Alaska Peninsula Glacier Complex would have precluded coastal migration because the ice extended beyond the continental shelf (Mann and Hamilton 1995). However, by 14,500 years BP, the ice had retreated to the extent that all but a few very small, scattered areas of the continental shelf along the Alaska coast, were exposed and ice-free. Along the British Columbia coast, by 15,000 years BP the ice had retreated, exposing the Queen Charlotte Islands, and all but a few isolated locales along the continental shelf. On the southwest British Columbia and Washington coasts, the Cordilleran Glacier Complex had retreated to expose Vancouver Island and the continental shelf by 14,000 years BP (Mann and Hamilton 1995).

To live in the Arctic, people must possess an extremely sophisticated sewing technology. This means, among other things, they have the ability to manufacture skin boats capable of traversing coastal waters. Given the circumstances at 14,500 years BP it is reasonable to assume that arctic residents were accomplished boat builders and users. Since by that time most of the land and water along the southeast coast of Alaska as well as the coasts of British Columbia and Washington were ice-free, the route and subsistence resources required to sustain a southward migration were available. It is worth remembering that at ca. 14,000 years BP, the geologic evidence suggests there was no ice-free corridor along the east flank of the Rocky Mountains (Mandryk et al. 1998; 2000).

Therefore, as early as 14,500 years BP, arctic immigrants, bearing big-game oriented economy and technology, could have worked their way south along the coast to a point in temperate North America where the coastal mountain ranges did not contain glacial barriers to the interior. Although supporting archaeological evidence from along the route is meager at best, the lack of evidence can, to a large extent, be explained by the substantial rise in sea level, which has flooded the coastal lands that were used by the late Pleistocene immigrants (Fladmark 1979; Easton 1992; Mann and Hamilton 1995). Since travel by boat is much more efficient and faster than travel by pedestrian means, southward migration by watercraft could get the arctic immigrants into temperate North America and into South America quickly and almost simultaneously (Kunz and Slaughter 2001).

SUMMARY

Most aspects of the Mesa research are relatively straightforward. The site was easy to excavate and document because in all of its localities except one, there is but a single cultural component. In other words, from the surface to the bottom of the soil column it is all one cultural unit. This allowed us to excavate without being too concerned about postdepositional mechanics within the active layer, which is always a problem in the shallow arctic Alaskan sites. The Mesa Complex artifact assemblage is uniform across the site. It is composed of just a few types of formal artifacts and is uncomplicated. The cultural features are all hearths, physically discrete and easily identifiable. The radiocarbon chronology is extensive and consistent across the site with few outliers, none of which are inexplicable. The technological attributes, manufacturing processes, tool types and morphology are unequivocally Paleoindian, and identify the Mesa lithic assemblage as a component of the Paleoindian tradition. Lastly, the lithic tool assemblage, as well as the geomorphology of the site demonstrates without question, that the site was used as a hunting lookout. While all these data provide us with a lot of answers, more questions are posed that require answers if we are to paint a complete picture of the Mesa and the people who used it.

Dan Mann's extensive and intensive work has provided an excellent look at the dynamics of climate and environment in the region from the last millennia of the Pleistocene through the onset of the Holocene (Kunz and Mann 1997, Kunz et al. 1999b; Mann et al. 2001; Mann et al. 2002). This work includes the examination and analysis of numerous geologic sections, including lake bottom sediments, which provide a chronology based on more than 60 radiocarbon assays of terrestrial plant remains. His work also examines pollen profiles, lake productivity data, and information concerning fluvial and near-surface soil dynamics. Among the other important results of this work, the existence of the Younger Dryas event in arctic Alaska was documented and confirmed. It is the Younger Dryas event that is most critical to the utilization of the area by Paleoindians.

In preceding sections of this report it has been demonstrated that shortly after the Last Glacial Maximum, global climate began to alter. As the climate in the region became warmer and wetter the habitat began to change, moving in the direction of moist tussock-tundra. As this change occurred it had two primary effects: relatively good forage was replaced with vegetation of considerably different nutritional value, and at the same time a soft, wet and tussocky surface was replacing a firm, dry, and relatively even surface on the landscape. This surface change made it increasingly difficult for the large herbivores to maintain the degree of mobility they required for viability. The first casualties appear to have been mammoth and horse, probably because they were the most grass-dependent species. During most of this period, the annual temperature was several degrees warmer than today, and the rate of change rapidly gained momentum. By 11,000 years BP, although a fair amount of the Pleistocene steppe-tundra probably remained, it was broken into relatively small chunks separated by large expanses of tussock-tundra. As a result, the carrying capacity of the region was greatly reduced, even for the more adaptable and versatile bison, and their numbers also went into decline. Fortunately for the human population of the area, the Younger Dryas event occurred, resulting in a climatic reversal to full glacial conditions, which maintained the remaining full glacial habitat along with its reduced bison population for the next millennium or so.

Paul Matheus' in-depth examination of the late Pleistocene faunal assemblage of the region provides a considerable body of data including species variety, stable isotope analysis, and species density chronology (Matheus 1998, 2000; Kunz et al. 1999b). This work shows that when the Mesa was occupied, game animal populations were lower than they had been in many millennia. From a subsistence standpoint, bison were probably the most reliable resource for the human inhabitants of arctic Alaska at that time, but they were by no means numerous. The people living in that region during that time had to take advantage of every opportunity to acquire game animals, and the best way to do that was to operate from a position that permitted surveillance of a large area, and at the same time rapid access to any location within the field of view. Locations like the Mesa were perfect for this type of hunting, as is demonstrated by other Mesa Complex sites in the region such as Hilltop (Reanier 1995), Putu/Bedwell (Reanier 1995), Spein Mountain (Ackerman 2001), and Kuna Bluff (Kunz 2001b). The fact that these types of sites were a critical aspect of the hunting process during terminal Pleistocene times, is demonstrated by their near total lack of use by groups that subsequently inhabited the region. Further evidence of the marginal nature of these circumstances, is the abandonment of the region by the Paleoindians ca. 9700 years BP, shortly after bison disappear from the fossil record. Additionally, the regional archaeological record indicates that people did not return to the region until ca. 7500 years BP, by which time, according to our data, caribou had once again become numerous in the Brooks Range and on the North Slope.

Life at the Mesa

Without getting ourselves bogged down in further examination of the research data, the following sketch is how we think the people using the Mesa were conducting their daily lives 12,000 to 10,000 radiocarbon years (14,000 to 12,000 calendar years) ago.

The Mesa people probably utilized the site most frequently from May through September. If they used it during the winter, it wasn't very often, and certainly not during the heart of the winter. This surmise is partly based on our own experience, having spent long periods in the region of the Mesa during all seasons of the year. The frequent high wind events of summer (see page 9) also occur during winter and would, in addition to other factors, have made use of the Mesa unattractive much of the time. Try to imagine what it would be like during the depths of the winter, occupying an exposed location like the Mesa. Day after day, you would have to cope with 24-hour darkness and temperatures well below zero. Often the wind would be in excess of 40 miles per hour, with blowing snow obscuring what little could otherwise be seen. Our best guess is that during the winter (October through April), most of the time the residents of the region were hunkered down in the more sheltered valleys of the Brooks Range.

Although we have no hard data to support this, we assume that the Mesa people's summer dwellings were dome-shaped tents comprised of a willow framework, over which animal hides were stretched. Rocks or blocks of sod, as well as stakes, were probably placed around the base of the structure to hold the skins in place. The dwellings were probably between eight and twelve feet in diameter, the floors lined with willow boughs, moss, and lichen. People

Figure 38. Nunamiut winter camp, 1910. (Photo: Leffingwell, U.S.G.S. Photographic Library.)

Our research has shown that the Mesa was not a habitation site. However, we believe that when the Mesa was in use, there was a base camp established along nearby Iteriak Creek. The riparian habitat along the creek provided all the resources (wood for fuel and construction, tool stone, good water, small game, fowl, and fish) necessary to sustain a fully functional camp. The size of the camp, as well as its location on the creek, probably varied, but the camp was always located so that the Mesa was easily accessible. We doubt that the camp population ever exceeded more than one or two dozen individuals, probably representing several generations of people related through blood and marriage.

probably slept on animal skins laid directly on the flooring. Dry willow provided the fuel for fires both inside and outside the shelter, although animal fat/oil lamps may also have been used.

It is likely that all adults could successfully perform any task. Given the self-sufficiency required to survive in the Arctic, men were probably as accomplished at sewing, as women were at making and using stone tools and hunting equipment. However, based on ethnohistoric and historic information regarding arctic aboriginal peoples, we assume that usually men and older boys were the hunters, and climbed the Mesa on a daily basis to keep a lookout for game. We think this was done because game animal populations were low at that time, and a vantage point such as the Mesa was the most efficient way to locate game. While looking for game from the top of the Mesa, the hunters worked on their equipment, repairing and refurbishing it. This work produced the numerous hearth-centered activity areas that our excavations revealed. Most of the stone these people utilized in their tool-making activities came from the Iteriak Creek gravels and other chert sources/outcrops within a few miles of the Mesa, so obtaining raw material was quick and easy. When game was spotted, the hunters would probably discuss the situation. If it was determined there was a reasonable chance to conduct a successful hunt, then they would plan the attack strategy. The Mesa was used prior to the time that tussock tundra completely covered the landscape. The surface of the land was more suited for walking in those days, and a hunter's effective range was probably greater than it is today. When a hunt was successful, the meat and hide would be taken to the camp for processing. Only on extremely rare occasions was meat cooked atop the Mesa.

Our research suggests that between 12,000 and 10,000 years BP, bison were the most numerous game animals, and most likely the primary target of the Mesa hunters. Although low in numbers, caribou, muskox, and moose were present as well. It is also probable that a few horses were still around, although mammoths appear to be absent from the North Slope by this time.

We also think that the Mesa hunters used dogs to help them in their hunts, primarily for packing, but also for harassing game. In fact, dogs were probably quite important to the nomadic Mesa people because they were the only domesticated beast of burden (pack animal) of that time. As far as we know, sleds had not yet been invented, so dogs were not being used in that fashion. Dogs were also the camp alarm system, and the initial responders to the approach of large predators, such as lions and bears, which were native to the region.

Although the climate and surface vegetation of the region at the end of the Pleistocene was somewhat different than it has been since that time, the resources available to the Mesa people were pretty much the same as those available today. Therefore, we think that the way the prehistoric/historic Nunamiut (inland) Eskimo conducted their daily and seasonal lives is generally a good analog for the Mesa peoples' lifestyle (Figure 38 & 39). For more information about the Nunamiut Eskimo see Helge Ingstad's, "Nunamiut: Among Alaska's Inland Eskimos" (1954) and Nicholas Gubser's, "The Nunamiut Eskimo: Hunters of Caribou" (1965).

Figure 39. Nunamiut Eskimoes moving camp, 1910. (Photo: Leffingwell, U.S.G.S. Photographic Library.)

GLOSSARY

AEOLIAN. A term referring to the transportation and deposition of fine grained soil, sand, or silt (such as loess) by wind. This process is responsible for the morphology of much of the landscape in northern and arctic Alaska.

ALLUVIATION. A process of depositing sand, silt, gravel and other water-transportable materials on the banks of, or in the bed of a stream or river—an alluvial deposit—an alluvial fan.

AMS RADIOCARBON DATING. The most precise method of determining the age of organic material recovered from archaeological or paleontological deposits. AMS stands for Accelerator Mass Spectrometry. This procedure, which operates at the atomic level to determine the amount of C-14 present in a sample, allows the analysis of a sample up to 1000 times smaller than the amount required for radiocarbon assays by the conventional method. (See Conventional Radiocarbon (C-14) Dating).

ASSAYED. A term meaning tested or analyzed.

ATLATL. Often referred to as a throwing-stick. This usually wooden tool is about two feet in length and not much more than an inch in width. The forward end is gripped by the hand, while the other end has a small, raised protrusion, nub, or hook which fits into a depression in the end of a dart or spear shaft. The hand-held atlatl actually launches the dart or spear. In essence, the atlatl increases the length of the user's arm, giving the arm more leverage (increasing its mechanical advantage), which in turn adds velocity, force, distance, and accuracy to the throw.

ATMOSPHERIC C-14. A radioactive isotope of carbon present in the atmosphere, and subsequently present in all living things. When an organism dies it ceases to absorb C-14 and, like any radioactive element, the C-14 within the organism begins to decay. The rate of decay is known and can be measured. For example, the amount of C-14 that is present in a mammoth bone today, when measured against the original amount, indicates how long ago the animal died, and therefore how old the bone is.

BIOTA. Plants and animals populating a geographic region.

BLADE. A blade is a specific type of stone flake. By definition, it has parallel sides and is at least twice as long as it is wide. Most often, a blade is derived from a core that has been prepared so that it will repetitively produce blades (flakes) of uniform size and shape. A blade is detached from the core by the force of either a percussion blow or pressure (also see Flake Core). The term blade can also refer to the body of a knife, biface, or projectile point.

BP. An abbreviation that means 'Before Present', but in reality means before 1950, which is the base year from which all radiocarbon measurements are made.

BURIN. A chisel-like stone tool. It is most commonly made by removing a slender flake (burin spall) along the length of the margin of one or more intersecting edges of a large flake. The edge(s) and sharp point formed by this process makes a tool ideal for scraping, shaping or engraving bone, antler, or wood.

CHANNEL MIGRATION. This refers to the side-to-side (meandering) movement of a stream channel within its flood plain over time.

COMEDIAL FLAKING. One of a variety of flake removal techniques utilized in the production of stone tools. Comedial flaking is most commonly employed in the manufacture of projectile points. It is the controlled removal of horizontal, parallel flakes from the surface of a stone tool, through the application of either percussion or pressure. Flakes removed from one edge meet the flakes removed from the other edge at the midline of the blade. This leaves a distinctive flake scar pattern and a medial ridge. If this type of flake removal is utilized on both surfaces it will produce a projectile point with a diamond or lenticular cross section. This method is also known as collateral flaking.

CONCHOIDAL FRACTURE. The predictable manner in which fine-grained stone such as flint, chert or obsidian fractures when struck. This physical property is basic to the controlled removal of flakes from a piece of stone, and is necessary for the manufacture of many types of stone tools. The name is derived from the physical appearance of the flake, which is often rippled on the surface and convex in cross section, somewhat resembling a clam shell.

CONVENTIONAL RADIOCARBON (C-14) DATING. A method of arriving at the age of organic material by determining the amount of C-14 remaining in that material (See Atmospheric C-14). The age is determined by actually counting the number of decay events that occur in the sample over a measured period of time. It is the original process for determining C-14 ages. This method requires a much larger sample and is less precise than the AMS procedure.

CORTEX. The outside surface or 'skin' of a nodule, cobble, or chunk of tool stone. The cortex is commonly worn, oxidized or weathered to a rough texture and often is a different color than the stone beneath it. The initial stage of most stone tool manufacture is the removal of cortex.

CRYOTURBATION. This term refers to disturbance or movement of objects within the soil column that results from freezing and thawing of the soil. This is generally attributed to seasonal freezing and thawing events, and is often referred to as 'frost heaving'.

CULTURAL MATERIAL. This term usually refers to physical material—such as stone tools and flakes, organic trash, campfire remnants, or structural remains—associated with, or the byproduct of, the occupation or use of a locale by humans.

CULTURAL STRATIGRAPHY. A description of how cultural material is arranged or layered within the soil (geological stratigraphy) of an archaeological site.

DEBITAGE. The waste material (flakes, chips, chunks) resulting from stone tool manufacture.

DETRITUS. The loose material or fragments that result from disintegration of the parent material. Detritus is often used interchangeably with the term debitage.

DRAG FLOAT. Typically a flotation device (in prehistoric times an inflated animal bladder or skin) attached to a harpoon line. Its function is to tire the harpooned animal, and to keep it from diving when alive, or sinking after death.

EVAPOTRANSPIRATION. A term referring to the loss of water from the soil that results from direct evaporation, as well as the water vapor given off by plants through their leaves.

FAUNAL ASSEMBLAGE. Usually refers to a suite of animal remains (most commonly bones) representing the variety of animals found within an archaeological or paleontological site, or a geographical area.

FLAKE CORE. Piece of tool stone which served as the source (core) for the production of large amorphous flakes. Tools were usually made from the flakes.

FORMAL ARTIFACT. A tool or tool fragment recognized as being purposely made to perform a specific task. Examples would be a projectile point, a knife, or a microblade core. A retouched flake, which is an incidental tool or tool of the moment, would not be included in this class of artifacts.

FROST CRACK. A crack in the soil caused by the expansion of water freezing within the soil column. Such a crack is usually identifiable on the surface of the ground as an indentation and/or marked by a concentration of vegetation somewhat different than that which surrounds it. The crack descends below the surface and may contain ice or soil if the ice has melted. Often the soil that has migrated into a frost crack will carry other material (such as artifacts) with it and be of a different character than the soil surrounding the crack.

GABBRO SUBSTRATE. The gabbro base on which the active soil zone at the Mesa is perched. Gabbro is a type of igneous rock. The substrate at the Mesa is composed of fractured gabbro bedrock ranging from granular to boulder-sized chunks.

GENERA. Plural form of genus, a biological classification marked by common characteristics. Genus falls between Family and Species in the classification hierarchy.

HAFT. A tool handle. It can also refer to attaching a handle to a tool (hafting), or a tool with a handle (hafted).

HAFTING. A process whereby a tool is secured to a handle or shaft. For example, by wrapping with sinew, gluing, or placing in a slot or groove.

HEARTH. The remains of an ancient campfire.

HEARTH FILL. Material found within the boundaries of an ancient campfire. This can include anything that fell or was thrown into the fire such as artifacts and food debris as well as charcoal and ash.

HINGE FRACTURE. This occurs during stone tool manufacture and is one of the ways a flake can terminate as it detaches from its core. Rather than feathering out (becoming thinner along its length until it detaches) the flake hinges out, the fracture turning sharply upward at its point of detachment creating a rounded 'hinge' at the distal end of the flake.

HOLOCENE. A geologic time period encompassing about the last 10,000 years.

HUMIC ACID. An acid formed in peaty soils. Humic acid breaks up clay and compacted soils, and helps to transfer micronutrients from soil to the plant. It can cause a brownish residue to be deposited in the soil, on rocks, and in water.

IN SITU. Refers to an object being in its natural or original position or place. This term is usually used in reference to the cultural material in an archaeological site in the sense that the material has been undisturbed since the site was abandoned (since the material was incorporated into the site's stratigraphy).

INFRARED SPECTROSCOPY. A method of mapping the components of a substance using infrared light in order to determine its chemical composition.

LENTICULAR. Refers to something having the shape of a double convex lens. This is a descriptive term usually applied to the cross sectional profile of a stone projectile point.

LITHIC. Relating to, or being of, stone. This term often refers to stone tools and the chips and flakes resulting from their manufacture.

LOESS. A very fine-grained silt-like material—often referred to as rock-flour—resulting from rock grinding during glacial activity. This material is usually carried away from a glacier by meltwater streams and deposited along the banks, or in fans or bars. Once dry it is often picked up by the wind and redeposited (aeolian deposition) miles beyond the limits of the stream. Loess deposits can be hundreds of feet thick.

MEGAFAUNA. Generally a collectively descriptive term for large animals. In an archaeological context it often refers to large mammals that lived during the Pleistocene, but became extinct when the ice age ended.

MORPHOLOGY. Form and/or structure. Herein, it is used in reference to the shape or appearance of a stone tool or artifact.

OBSIDIAN. Volcanic glass. Obsidian was often used as a tool stone. Tools that are made from obsidian are sharper, but more brittle, than tools made of flint or chert.

OBSIDIAN HYDRATION DATING. A method of determining the age of obsidian, usually an obsidian artifact. Like all glass, obsidian absorbs moisture from its environment. Because the moisture is absorbed at a known rate, measuring the amount of water that has been absorbed by an obsidian tool since it was made will establish the tool's age. There are a number of locally variable factors that influence the rate of moisture absorption. These must be known and factored into the equation, if the resulting date is to be considered reliable.

PALEOECOLOGY. The study of the characteristics of ancient environments and their relationships with the animals and plants that occupied them.

PERMAFROST. A permanently frozen layer of soil and/or rock of varying thickness occurring primarily in the Arctic and Antarctic.

PHYTOLITHS. Microscopic forms of silicates found in plant matter. Phytoliths can be found as deposits on the teeth of animals that eat plants or on tools that are used to cut the plants. Because phytoliths are plant specific, the type of phytoliths found on teeth or tools identify the types of plants being eaten or utilized.

PLEISTOCENE. A geologic time period beginning about 1.6 million years ago, and ending about 10,000 years ago, commonly referred to as the ice age.

PLEISTOCENE / HOLOCENE TRANSITION. A period of several thousand years that spans the changing of the climate at the end of the ice age to conditions more like the present.

PROVENIENCE. The location of a site, or object within a site, determined by geographic coordinates or directional/distance measurement from a known point.

RADIO REPEATER SYSTEM. A system in which two or more stationary radio receiver and transmitter pairs are arrayed in order to facilitate long distance radio communication.

RADIOCARBON DATING. A method for determining the age of organic material. Because of its presence in the atmosphere, a small amount of C-14, the radioactive isotope of carbon, is found in all living things. On the death of an organism, C-14 decays at a known rate (its half-life is 5730 years). When the amount of C-14 in dead organic material is measured, it indicates the length of time that has passed since the organism died. For example, a bison bone is found in an archaeological site with an stone arrow head imbedded in it. In the laboratory, a C-14 assay is done on the bison bone and returns an age of 4850 +/- 90 yrs. BP. As a result the archaeologist can infer that the prehistoric hunting camp was occupied at the same time the bison was killed—4850 radiocarbon years BP.

RADIOCARBON YEARS. A descriptive term of radiocarbon age. Radiocarbon years are based on the decay rate of C-14, and are not the same as calendar years. Generally speaking, the older the radiocarbon age is, the greater the disparity between it and calendar years. For example, there would only be a slight disparity between radiocarbon and calendar years if the radiocarbon age is 1500 yrs. BP—the calendar year age would be about 1580 years ago. If the radiocarbon age was 10,000 years BP, the calendar age would be about 12,150 years ago. Conversion/calibration curves addressing the difference between these two systems have been developed using tree-ring, Greenland ice-core, and other data. Most archaeological and paleontological dates are reported in radiocarbon years. There are limits to radiocarbon dating, and the accuracy of age determinations in excess of 50,000 years BP is highly questionable.

RETOUCH. A rather general term that can cover most types of modification to a stone tool beyond its initial stages of manufacture. Most often the term refers to the removal of small flakes from the edges or surfaces of a stone tool to aid in final shaping and/or sharpening. Retouch may be unifacial—occurring on only one surface of the tool, or bifacial—occurring on both surfaces of the tool.

RIPARIAN. An ecological zone occurring adjacent to stream courses. Usually this zone is contained within the limits of the active and inactive flood plains of the stream. However, with large watercourses this zone may extend beyond those limits.

SEMI-SUBTERRANEAN HOUSE. An archaeological term describing a dwelling of which at least the lower one-third has been excavated into the ground. This type of dwelling is often referred to as a "pit house".

SEXUAL DIMORPHISM. Differences usually referring to color or size between the males and females of a species. For instance, in many species, males are larger than females.

SOLIFLUCTION. A term referring to the slow downslope movement of thawed, moisture laden soil sliding on a buried surface of frozen material. This usually occurs at the contact point of the active (thawed) soil zone and permafrost. Often the soil and surface vegetation are bound together, and much like a carpet, move downslope as a single unit.

TAXA. The plural form of the term taxon, which is a group of plants or animals designated in a formal system of nomenclature.

TOOL STONE. A stone that has a very fine crystal structure (crypto crystalline), and possesses the property of conchoidal fracture. Such material is ideal for making flaked stone tools. Flint, chert, obsidian, and basalt are examples of this type of stone.

TUSSOCK TUNDRA. A treeless landscape that is found in arctic and subarctic regions. It is populated by dwarf shrubs, mosses, lichens, and herbs, and dominated by compact tussocks or tufts of grass or sedges. This type of tundra is often moist or wet during the summer, and underlain by a dark, mucky soil perched on permafrost.

TYPOLOGY. As used herein, a method of arranging artifacts according to classes or types.

UPPER PALEOLITHIC. Generally speaking, the last 40,000 years of the Old Stone Age— approximately 50,000–10,000 years BP.

USE-WEAR. Evidence of wear on stone tools that occurs as the result of the use of the tool.

YOUNGER DRYAS. Time period spanning roughly 1000 years, between 11,000 and 10,000 radiocarbon years ago.

REFERENCES CITED

Ackerman, R.E.
   2001   Spein Mountian: A Mesa Complex Site in Southwestern Alaska.
   Arctic Anthropology 38(2).

Adkins, C.E.
   1994   Mesa 44-40 W.C.F. Manuscript on file with the Bureau of Land
   Management, Northern Field Office, Fairbanks, Alaska.

Adovasio, J.M. and R.C. Carlisle, eds
   1982   Meadowcroft: Collected Papers on the Archaeology of Meadowcroft
   Rockshelter and the Cross Creek Drainage. Prepared for the 47th Annual
   Meeting of the Society of American Archaeology, Minneapolis, Minnesota.

Alley, R.B.
   2000   The Younger Dryas cold interval as viewed from central Greenland.
   Quaternary Science Reviews 19: 213-226.

Alley, R.B. and 10 others
   1993   Abrupt increase in Greenland snow accumulation at the end of
   the Younger Dryas event. *Nature* 362: 527-529.

Amick, D. S. and R. P. Mauldin, eds
   1989   *Experiments in Lithic technology.* BAR International Series 528.

Anderson, D. D.
   1968   A stone age campsite at the gateway to America. *Scientific American*
   218(6):24-33.

   1970   Akmak: an early archaeological assemblage from Onion Portage,
   Nortwest Alaska. *Acta Arctica* Fasc. 16. Danish Arctic Institute, Copenhagen.

   1988   *Onion Portage: the archaeology of a stratified site from the Kobuk River
   in northwest Alaska.* Anthropological Papers of the University of Alaska
   22(1-2). University of Alaska Press, Fairbanks.

Anderson-Gerfaud, P.
   1990   Aspects of Behavior in the Middle Paleolithic: Functional Analysis of
   Stone Tools from Southwest France. In Paul Mellars (ed) *The Emergence of
   Modern Humans*, 389-418. Ithaca, New York: Cornell University Press.

Anderson, D.G. and J.C. Gillam
   2000   Paleoindian Colonization of the Americas: Implications from an
   Examination of Physiography, Demography, and Artifact Distribution.
   American Antiquity, 65 (1):43-66.

Beikman, H.M. and E.H. Lathram
   1976   Preliminary Geologic Map of Northern Alaska. *Miscellaneous Field
   Studies Map* MF-789, U.S. Geological Survey, Washington, D.C.

Bever, M.R.
   2000   *Paleoindian Lithic Technology and Landscape Use in Late Pleistocene
   Alaska: A Study of the Mesa Complex.* PhD. Dissertation, Department of
   Anthropology, Southern Methodist University, Dallas, Texas.

Binford, L.R.
1978 *Nunamiut Ethnoarchaeology*. Academic Press, New York.

1980 Willow Smoke and Dog's Tails: Hunter-Gatherer Settlement Systems and Archaeological Site Formation. *American Antiquity* 45(1):4-20.

Björck, S., B. Kromer, S. Johnsen, O. Bennike, D. Hammarlund, G. Lendahl, G. Possnert, T.L. Rasmussen, B. Wohlfarth, C.U. Hammer, , and M. Spurk.
1996 Synchronized terrestrial-atmospheric deglacial records around the North Atlantic: Science 274, 1155-1160.

Boast, R.B.
1983 *The Folsom Gravers: A Functional Determination Through Microwear Analysis*. Masters thesis, Department of Anthropology, University of Colorado, Boulder, Colorado.

Bockstoce, J.R.
1976 On the Development of Whaling in the Western Thule Culture. *Folk* 18:41-46.

1986 *Whales, Ice, and Men: The History of Steam Whaling in the Western Arctic*. University of Washington Press. Seattle.

Boldurian, A.T. and J.L. Cotter
1999 *Clovis Revisited: New Perspectives on Paleoindian Adaptations from Blackwater Draw, New Mexico*. The University Museum, University of Pennsylvania, Philadelphia.

Bowers, P.M.
1982 The Lisburne Site: analysis and culture history of a multi-component lithic workshop in the Iteriak Valley, Arctic foothills, Northern Alaska. *Anthropological Papers of the University of Alaska* 20(1):79-112.

1999 AMS dating of the Area 22 American PaleoArctic tradition microblade component at the Lisburne site, Arctic Alaska. *Current Research in the Pleistocene* 16.

Bradley, B.A.
1993 Paleo-Indian Flaked Stone Technology in the North American High Plains. In *From Kostenki to Clovis: Upper Paleolithic – Paleo-Indian Adaptations*. Edited by O. Soffer and N. Praslov, pp. 251-262. Plenum Press, New York.

Brower, C.D.
1942 *Fifty Years Below Zero: A Lifetime of Adventure in the Far North*. Dodd, Mead and Company, New York.

Campbell, J.M.
1968 Territoriality Among Ancient Hunters: Interpretations from Ethnography and Nature. In *Archaeology of the Americas*. Anthropological Society of Washington, pp. 1-21.

Carter, L.D.
1993 Late Pleistocene stabilization and reactivation of eolian sand in northern Alaska: implications for the effects of future climatic warming on an aeolian landscape in continuous permafrost. In *Proceedings, Sixth International Conference on Permafrost, Beijing, China*. South China University Technology Press, Wushan, Guangzhou, China volume 1, pp. 78-83.

Chapman, R.M., R.L. Detterman, and M.D. Mangus
    1964   *Geology of the Killik-Etivluk Rivers Region, Alaska.* Geological Survey
Professional Paper 303-F. U.S. Geological Survey, Washington D.C.

Clark, D.W.
    1991   The northern (Alaska-Yukon) fluted points. In *Clovis: origins and
adaptations*, edited by R. Bonnichsen and K.L. Turnmire, pp. 35-48. Center
for the Study of the First Americans, Corvallis 38(2).

    2001   Microblade-culture Systematics in the Far Interior Northwest.
Arctic Anthropology 38(2).

Clark, D.W. and A.M. Clark
    1975   Fluted points from the Batza Téna obsidian source of the Koyukuk
River region Alaska. *Anthropological Papers of the University of Alaska*
17(2):31-38.

    1983   Paleo-Indians and fluted points: Subarctic alternatives. *Plains
Anthropologist* 28:283-292.

    1993   *Batza Téna: Trail to obsidian.* Canadian Museum of Civilization,
Quebec.

Collins, H. B.
    1937   Notes and news: Arctic area. *American Antiquity* 3:188.

Collins, M.B
    1999   *Clovis Blade Technology: A Comparative Study of the Keven Davis
Cache, Texas.* University of Texas Press, Austin.

Cook, H. J.
    1927   New geological and palaeontological evidence bearing on the antiquity
of mankind in America. *Natural History* 27:240-247.

Cook, J.P.
    1969   The early prehistory of Healy Lake, Alaska. Ph.D. dissertation.
University of Wisconsin, Madison. University Microfilms, Ann Arbor.

    1999 Blade and Core Technology in Alaska. Paper presented at the 64th
Annual Meeting of the Society For American Archaeology, Chicago, Illinois.

De Laguna, Frederica
    1936   An archaeological reconnaissance of the middle and lower Yukon
Valley, Alaska. *American Antiquity* 2:6-12.

Dikov, N.N.
    1977   Archaeological monuments of Kamchatka, Chukotka, and the Upper
Kolyma. Nauka, Moscow

    1979   Ancient Cultures of Northeast Asia. Nauka, Moscow.

    1996   The Ushki sites, Kamchatka Peninsula. In *American beginnings: the
prehistory and paleoecology of Beringia*, edited by F.H. West, pp. 244-250.
The University of Chicago Press, Chicago.

1997 *Asia at the Juncture with America in antiquity: The stone age of the Chukchi Peninsula.* U.S. Department of the Interior, National Park Service, Beringia Program, Anchorage, Alaska. Translated from the Russian (1993) by Richard L. Bland.

Dillehay, T.D.
1997 *Monte Verde: A Late Pleistocene Settlement in Chile Volume 2: The Archaeological Context and Interpretation.* Smithsonian Institution Press, Washington, D.C.

Dumond, D.E
1980 The archaeology of Alaska and the peopling of America. *Science* 209:984-991.

1987 *The Eskimos and Aleuts.* Thames and Hudson Ltd., London.

Durand, S.R., R.E. Reanier, and D.H.Mann
1998 Archaeological and Geological Mapping on the North Slope. Manuscript and maps on file at the Bureau of Land Management, Northern Field Office, Fairbanks, Alaska.

Easton, N.A.
1992 Mal de mer above Terra Incognita, or, what ails the coastal migration theory? *Arctic Anthropology* 29(2):28-41.

Figgins, J.D.
1927 The Antiquity of Man in America. *Natural History* 27(3): 240-247.

Fladmark, K. R.
1979 Routes: alternate migration corridors for early man in North America. *American Antiquity* 44:55-69.

Foote, D.C.
1964 American Whalemen in Northwestern Arctic Alaska. *Arctic Anthropology* 2(2):16-20.

Frison, G.C.
1978 *Prehistoric Hunters of the High Plains.* Academic Press, New York.

1988 Paleoindian Subsistence and Settlement During Post-Clovis Times on the Northwestern Plains, the Adjacent Mountain Ranges, and Intermontane Basins. In: *Americans Before Columbus: Ice-Age Origins*, edited by Ronald C. Carlisle. Ethnology Monographs No. 12, Department of Anthropology, University of Pittsburg.

1991 *Prehistoric hunters of the High Plains.* Academic Press, New York.

Frison, G.C. and D.J. Stanford
1974 The Agate Basin Site: A Record of Paleoindian Occupation of the Northwestern High Plains. Academic Press, New York.

Fullagar, R.L.K.
1991 The Role of Silica in Polish Formation. *Journal of Archaeological Science* 18:1-24.

Gal, R.
1982   Excavations at the Tunalik Site, Northwestern National Petroleum Reserve in Alaska. *Anthropological Papers of the University of Alaska* 20(1):61-78.

Gerlach, S.C. and E.S. Hall Jr.
1988   The Later Prehistory of Northern Alaska: The View From Tukuto Lake. In: The Late Prehistoric Development of Alaska's Native People, edited by R.D. Shaw, R.K. Harritt, and D.E. Dumond, pp. 107-135. Aurora, Alaska Anthropological Association Monograph Series No. 4.

Giddings, J.L. Jr.
1964   *The Archaeology of Cape Denbigh.* Brown University Press, Providence.

Giddings, J.L. and D.D. Anderson
1986   Beach Ridge Archaeology of Cape Krusenstern: Eskimo and Pre-Eskimo Settlements Around Kotzebue Sound, Alaska. Publication in Archaeology 20, National Park Service, U.S Department of the Interior, Washington, D.C.

Goebel, T., W.R. Powers, and N. Bigelow
1991   The Nenana Complex of Alaska and Clovis Origins. In *Clovis: Origins and Adaptations.* Robson Bonnichsen and Karen L. Turnmire eds. Center for the Study of the First Americans, Oregon State University, Corvallis.

Goebel, T., M. Waters, M. Dikova
2002   The Ushki Sites, Kamchatka and Pleistocene Peopling of the Americas. Paper presented at the 67th Annual Meeting of The Society for American Archaeology, Denver, Colorado.

Goslar, T., M. Arnold, N. Tisnerat-Laborde, J. Czernik, and K. Wieckowski
2000   Variations of Younger Dryas atmospheric radiocarbon without ocean circulation changes. *Nature* 403: 877-880.

Grootes, P.M. and Stuiver, M.
1997   Oxygen 18/16 variability in Greenland snow and ice with 10^3 to 10^5-year time resolution. *Journal of Geophysical Research* 102: 26,455 - 26,470.

Gubser, N.J.
1965   *The Nunamiut Eskimo: Hunters of Caribou.* Yale University Press, New Haven.

Guthrie, R.D.
1982   Mammals of the Mammoth Steppe as Paleoenvironmental Indicators. In D.M. Hopkins et al. eds., *Paleoecology of Beringia* 307-329. New York, Academic Press.

1990   *Frozen Fauna of the Mammoth Steppe.* Chicago, Illinois, University of Chicago Press.

Hajdas, I., G. Bonani, P. Bodén, D.M. Peteet, and D.H. Mann
1998   Cold reversal on Kodiak Island, Alaska, correlated with the European Younger Dryas using variations of atmospheric ^{14}C content. *Geology* 26: 1047-1050.

Hall, E.S. Jr.
  1961   Eskimo-Aleut Ethnobotany. MS on file, Department of Anthropology,
  Yale University, New Haven.

Hamilton, T.D.
  1986   Late Cenozoic glaciation of the central Brooks Range, in:
  Glaciation in Alaska (T.D. Hamilton, K.M. Reed, and R.M. Thorson, Eds.),
  pp. 9-50. Alaska Geological Society, Anchorage, Alaska.

Hardy, B.L.
  1994   *Investigation of Stone Tools Function through Use-wear, Residue, and
  DNA Analysis at the Middle Paleolithic Site of La Quina, France*. PhD.
  Dissertation, Indiana University.

  2000   Residue and Use-wear Analysis of Lithic Artifacts from the Mesa Site
  (KIR-102). Manuscript on file with the Bureau of Land Management,
  Northern Field Office, Fairbanks, Alaska.

  2001   Residue and Use-wear Analysis of Lithic Artifacts from the Mesa Site
  (KIR-102) sample #2. Manuscript on file with the Bureau of Land
  Management, Northern Field Office, Fairbanks, Alaska.

Hardy, B.L. and G.T. Garufi
  1998   Identification of Woodworking on Stone Tools through Residue and
  Use-wear Analysis: experimental results. Journal of Archaeological Science
  25:84-177.

Hardy, B.L. and M. Kay
  1998   Stone Tool Function at Starosele: combining Use-Wear and Residue
  Results. In V. Chabai and K. Monigal (eds), The Middle Paleolithic of the
  Western Crimea, Vol. 2. Liege:ERAUL, pp. 197-209.

Hinzman, L.D., D.L.Kane, C.S. Benson, and K.R. Everett
  1996   Energy balance and hydrological processes in an arctic watershed. In
  Landscape Function and Disturbance in Arctic Tundra (J.F. Reynolds and
  J.D. Tenhunen, Eds.) pp. 131-152. Springer Verlag, New York.

Hoffecker J.F.
  2001   Late Pleistocene and Holocene Sites in the Nenana Valley, Alaska.
  Arctic Anthropology 38(2).

Holmes, C. E.
  1996   Broken Mammoth. In *American beginnings: the prehistory and
  paleoecology of Beringia*, edited by F.H. West, pp. 312-318. The University of
  Chicago Press, Chicago.

  2001   Tanana Valley Archaeology Circa 12,000 to 8500 Yrs. BP.
  Arctic Anthropology 38(2).

Hopkins, D.M.
  1982   Aspects of the paleogeography of Beringia during the late
  Pleistocene. *In Paleoecology of Beringia* (D.M. Hopkins, J.V. Mathews, C.E.
  Schweger, and S.B. Young, Eds.), pp. 3-28. New York, Academic Press.

Howard, E. B.
  1936   The antiquity of man in America. *Scientific Monthly* 43:367-371.

Ingstad, H. M.
1954   *Nunamiut: Among Alaska's Inland Eskimoes.* Translated by F. H. Lyon. Allen Unwin, London.

Irving, W.N.
1964   Punyik Point and the Arctic Small Tool Tradition. PhD. Dissertation, University of Wisconsin, Madison. University Microfilms no. 64-10247.

Irwin, H.T. and H.M. Wormington
1970   Paleo-Indian Tool Types in the Great Plains. *American Antiquity* 35(1):24-34.

Isarin, R.F.B. and S.J.P. Bohncke
1999   Mean July temperatures during the Younger Dryas in northwestern and central Europe as inferred from climate indicator plant species. *Quaternary Research* 51: 158-173.

Judge, W.J.
1973   Paleoindian Occupation of the Central Rio Grande in New Mexico. University of New Mexico Press, Albuquerque.

Kane, D.L., L.D. Hinzman, M-K. Woo, and K.R. Everett
1992   Arctic Hydrology and Climate Change. in *Arctic Ecosystems in a Changing Climate, an Ecophysiological Perspective* (F.S. Chapin, R.L. Jeffries, J.F. Reynolds, G.R. Shaver, and J. Svoboda, Eds.), pp. 35-57. Academic Press, New York.

Kay, M.
1996   Microwear Analysis of some Clovis and Experimental Chipped Stone Tools. In G. Odell (ed), *Stone Tools: Theoretical Insights into Human Behavior*. New York: Plenum, pp. 315-344.

Kitigawa, H. and J. van der Plicht
1998   Atmospheric radiocarbon calibrations to 45,000 yr B.P.: Late Glacial fluctuations and cosmogenic isotope production. *Science* 279: 1187-1190.

Kunz, M.L.
1982   The Mesa Site: An Early Holocene Hunting Stand in the Iteriak Valley, Northern Alaska. *Anthropological papers of the University of Alaska* 20 (1-2): 113-122.

1991   *Cultural Resource Survey and Inventory: Gates of the Arctic National Park and Preserve, Alaska.* National Park Service, Alaska Region, Anchorage. Research/Resources Management Report AR-18.

1996   From the Arctic to the High Plains: Climate and Environmental Factors Influencing the Southward Movement of the Earliest North Americans. Paper presented at the 54th Annual Plains Anthropological Conference, Iowa City, Iowa.

1997   Passing Through Beringia: Speculation Concerning the Reasons Behind the Apparent Rapid Spread of Humans Throughout the Western Hemisphere. Paper presented at the 24th Annual Meeting of the Alaska Anthropological Association, Fairbanks, Alaska.

1998   The Good, The Bad, and the Ugly — Ancient Radiocarbon Dates, Chronologies, Mysteries, and Applications: a Paleoindian Example from Arctic Alaska. Paper presented at the 56th Annual Meeting of the Plains Anthropological Conference, Bismark, North Dakota.

2001a   Late Pleistocene Cultural Complexes in Eastern Beringia: The Best Bet for Clovis Progenitors. Paper presented at the 66th Annual Meeting of the Society For American Archaeology, New Orleans.

2001b   Kuna Bluff Site field notes. On file with the Bureau of Land Management, Northern Field Office, Fairbanks, Alaska.

Kunz, M.L. and D.H. Mann
1997   The Mesa Project: Interactions Between Early Prehistoric Humans and Environmental Change in Alaska. *Arctic Research of the United States*, 11:55-62.

Kunz, M.L. and P.G. Phippen
1988   An Early Nunamiut Campsite on Confusion Creek: Gates of the Arctic National Park, Alaska. Manuscript on file with Gate of the Arctic National Park, Fairbanks.

Kunz, M.L. and R.E. Reanier
1994   Paleoindians in Beringia: evidence from Arctic Alaska. *Science* 263:660-662.

1995   The Mesa site: a Paleoindian hunting lookout in Arctic Alaska. *Arctic Anthropology* 32:5-30.

Kunz, M.L., P.E. Matheus, D.H. Mann, and P. Groves
1999a   The Life and Times of Paleoindians in Arctic Alaska. *Arctic Research of the United States* 13: 33-39.

Kunz, M.L., P.E. Matheus, and D.H. Mann
1999b   Paleoindians and Bison in the Arctic: A High Plains Analog or a Different Story? Paper presented at the 57th Annual Meeting of the Plains Anthropological Conference, Sioux Falls, South Dakota.

2000 Environmental Determinism and Paleoindians in Arctic Alaska. Paper presented at the 65th Annual Meeting of the Society For American Archaeology, Philadelphia, Pennsyvania.

Kunz, M.L. and D.C. Slaughter
2001   Clovis and the Denbigh Flint Complex: Paleoindian Insights from Paleoeskimo Dynamics. Paper presented at the at the 59th Annual Meeting of the Plains Anthropological Conference, Lincoln, Nebraska.

Kunz, M.L., C.M. Adkins, and R.E. Reanier
2001   The Batza Téna Obsidian Source: Physical Description and Resource Availability. Paper presented at the 28th Annual Meeting of the Alaska Anthropological Association, Fairbanks, Alaska.

Loy, T.H. and E.J. Dixon
1998   Blood Residues on Fluted Points from Eastern Beringia. *American Antiquity* 63:24-35.

Lynch, T.F.
  1991   Paleoindians in South America: A Discrete and Identifiable Cultural
  Stage? In *Clovis Origins and Adaptations,* edited by Robson Bonnichsen and
  Karen L. Turnmire, pp.255-260. Peopling of the Americas, Oregon State
  University, Corvallis.

Mann, Daniel H. and Thomas D. Hamilton
  1995   Late Pleistocene and Holocene paleoenvironments of the North Pacific
  coast. *Quaternary Science Reviews* 14:449-471.

Mann, D.H., R.E. Reanier, D.M. Peteet, M.L. Kunz, and M. Johnson
  2001   Environmental Change and Paleoindians in Northern Alaska.
  Arctic Anthropology 38(2).

Mann, D.H., D.M. Peteet, R.E. Reanier, and M.L. Kunz
  2002   Responses of an Arctic Landscape to Late Glacial and Early
  Holocene Climate Changes: the Importance of Moisture. *Quaternary Science
  Reviews.*

Mandryk, C.A.S., H. Josenhans, D.W. Fedje, and R.W. Mathewes
  1998   Evaluating Paleoenvironmental Constraints on Interior and Coastal
  Entry Routes into North America. Paper presented at the 64th Annual
  Meeting of the Society For American Archaeology, Seattle Washington.

  2001   Late Quaternary Paleoenvironments of Northwestern North
  America: Implications for Inland vs. Coastal Migration Routes. *Quaternary
  Science Reviews.* (20) 1-3:301-314.

Martin, P.S. and R.G. Klein
  1984   *Quaternary Extinctions, a Prehistoric Revolution.* University of
  Arizona Press, Tucson, 892 pp.

Matheus, P.E.
  1998   Late Quaternary Mammal Fossils of the Ikpikpuk River, National
  Petroleum Reserve - Alaska. Draft manuscript on file with the Bureau of
  Land Management, Northern Field Office, Fairbanks, Alaska.

  2000   Late Quaternary Mammal Fossils of the Greater Ikpikpuk River Area,
  National Petroleum Reserve - Alaska. Draft manuscript on file with the
  Bureau of Land Management, Northern Field Office, Fairbanks, Alaska.

Mayewski, P.A., L.D. Meeker, S. Whitlow, M.S. Twickler, M.C. Morrison, R.B. Alley, and
  K. Taylor
  1993   The atmosphere during the Younger Dryas. *Science* 261: 195-197.

Mobley, Charles M.
  1991   *The Campus site: a prehistoric camp at Fairbanks, Alaska.* University
  of Alaska Press, Fairbanks.

Moritz, R.E.
  1979   *Synoptic climatology of the Beaufort Sea coast of Alaska.*
  Institute of Arctic and Alpine Research Occasional Paper Number 30, 176 pp.

Morrow, J.E. and T.A. Morrow
  1999   Geographic Variation in Fluted Projectile Points. *American Antiquity,*
  64 (2):215-230.

Mull, C.G.
 1994   The Geological Distribution of Chert in the Brooks Range. Paper presented at the 21st Alaska Anthropological Association Conference, Juneau, Alaska.

Nelson, N.C.
 1935   Early migration of man to America. *Natural History* 35:356.

 1937   Notes on cultural relationships between Asia and America. *American Antiquity* 2:267-272.

Newman, J.E. and C.I. Branton
 1972   Annual water balance and agricultural development in Alaska. *Ecology* 53: 513 519.

Patric, J.H. and Black, P.E.
 1968   Potential Evaporation and Climate in Alaska by Thornthwaite's Classification. *United States Department of Agriculture Forest Service Research Paper* PNW-71. Pacific Northwest Forest and Range Experimental Station, Institute of Northern Forestry, Juneau, Alaska.

Powers, W R.and J. F. Hoffecker
 1989   Late Pleistocene settlement in the Nenana Valley, Central Alaska. *American Antiquity* 54:263-287.

Powers, W R.and R.H. Jordan
 1990   Human Biogeography and Climate Change in Siberia and Arctic North America in the Fourth and Fifth Millennia BP. Phil. Trans. R. Soc, Lond A 330, 665-670.

Rainey, Froelich
 1939   *Archaeology in Central Alaska.* Anthropological Papers of the American Museum of Natural History 36:351-405.

 1940   Archaeological investigation in central Alaska. *American Antiquity* 4:299-308.

Rasic, J.T.
 2000   *Prehistoric Lithic Technology At The Tuluaq Hill Site, Northwest Alaska.* Masters thesis, Department of Anthropology, Washington State University, Pullman, Washington.

Reanier, R.E.
 1982   An Application of Pedological and Palynological Techniques at the Mesa Site. Northern Brooks Range, Alaska. *Anthropological Papers of the University of Alaska* 20(1-2):123-139.

 1995   The antiquity of Paleoindian Materials in Northern Alaska. *Arctic Anthropology* 32: 31-50.

 1996   Analysis of Hearth Charcoal from the Mesa Archaeological Site. Draft manuscript on File with the Bureau of Land Management, Fairbanks, Alaska.

 1997   Regional Culture History and Prehistoric Sites 10,000 B.C. to 1,500 A.D. In: NPR-A Symposium Proceedings: Science, Traditional Knowledge, and the Resources of the Northeast Planning Area of the National Petroleum Reserve Alaska. Minerals Management Service, OCS Study MMS 97-0013. Anchorage, Alaska.

Roberts, F.H.H. Jr.
1940   Developments in the Problem of the North American Paleo-Indian. Smithsonian Miscellaneous, Vol. 100. Washington, D.C.

Rovansek, R.J., L.D. Hinzman, and D.L. Kane
1996   Hydrology of a tundra wetland complex on the Alaska Arctic Coastal Plain, USA. Arctic and Alpine Research 28, 311-317.

Sanger, D.
1970   Mid-Latitude Core and Blade Traditions. *Arctic Anthropology* (7) 2:106-114.

Schoenberg, K. M.
1995   The Post-Paleoarctic Interval in the Central Brooks Range. *Arctic Anthropology* 32(1):51-62.

Sellet, F.
1999   A dynamic view of Paleoindian assemblages at the Hell Gap site, Wyoming: reconstructing lithic technological systems. Unpublished Ph.D. dissertation. Department of Anthropology, Southern Methodist University, Dallas Texas.

2001   A Changing Perspective on Paleoindian Chronology and Typology: A View From the Northwestern Plains. *Arctic Anthropology* 38(2).

Sheehan, G.W.
1997   The Most Successful Hunters: Northern Economy A.D. 400 to Present. In: NPR-A Symposium Proceedings: Science, Traditional Knowledge, and the Resources of the Northeast Planning Area of the National Petroleum Reserve Alaska. Minerals Management Service, OCS Study MMS 97-0013. Anchorage, Alaska.

Shelley, P.H.
1994   Views on the Mesa Site Lithic Resource Availability and Lithic Technology. Manuscript on file with the Bureau of Land Management, Northern Field Office, Fairbanks, Alaska.

Slobodin, S.B. and M.L. King
1996   Uptar and Kheta: Upper Paleolithic sites of the upper Kolyma Region. In *American beginnings: the prehistory and paleoecology of Beringia*, edited by F.H. West, pp. 236-244. The University of Chicago Press, Chicago.

Spetzman, L.A.
1959   *Vegetation of the Arctic Slope of Alaska*. Professional Paper 302-B. U.S. Geological Survey, Washington D.C.

Stanford, D.J.
1976   The Walakpa site, Alaska: Its Place in the Birnirk and Thule cultures. Contributions to Anthropology no. 20. Smithsonian Institution Press, Washington D.C..

Straus, G.L.
2000   Solutrean Settlement of North America? A Review of Reality. *American Antiquity* 65 (2):219-226.

Troeng, J.
    1993   Worldwide Chronology of Fifty-three Prehistoric Inovations. *Acta Archaeologica Lundensia*, Series in 8° . No 21.

Watson, R.
    1999   A Vegetation Study at the Mesa Site in Northern Alaska. Manuscript on file at the Bureau of Land Management, Northern Field Office, Fairbanks, Alaska.

West, F.H.
    1981   *The archaeology of Beringia.* Columbia University Press, New York.

Wormington, H.M.
    1957   *Ancient man in North America.* Denver Museum of Natural History, Denver.

Zhang, T., T.E. Osterkamp, and K. Stamnes
    1997   Effects of climate on the active layer and permafrost on the North Slope of Alaska, U.S.A. Permafrost and Periglacial Processes 8, 45-67.